CAMBRIDGE STUDIES IN PHILOSOPHY

Self-Concern

CAMBRIDGE STUDIES IN PHILOSOPHY

General editor ERNEST SOSA (Brown University)

Advisory editors:
JONATHAN DANCY (University of Reading),
JOHN HALDANE (University of St. Andrews),
GILBERT HARMAN (Princeton University),
FRANK JACKSON (Australian National University),
WILLIAM G. LYCAN (University of North Carolina at Chapel Hill),
SYDNEY SHOEMAKER (Cornell University),
JUDITH J. THOMSON (Massachusetts Institute of Technology)

Self-Concern

AN EXPERIENTIAL APPROACH TO
WHAT MATTERS IN SURVIVAL

Raymond Martin
University of Maryland, College Park

CAMBRIDGE
UNIVERSITY PRESS

PUBLISHED BY THE PRESS SYNDICATE OF THE UNIVERSITY OF CAMBRIDGE
The Pitt Building, Trumpington Street, Cambridge CB2 1RP, United Kingdom

CAMBRIDGE UNIVERSITY PRESS
The Edinburgh Building, Cambridge CB2 2RU, United Kingdom
40 West 20th Street, New York, NY 10011-4211, USA
10 Stamford Road, Oakleigh, Melbourne 3166, Australia

First published 1998

Printed in the United States of America

Typeset in Bembo

Library of Congress Cataloging-in-Publication Data
Martin, Raymond, 1941–
Self-concern : an experiential approach to what matters in
survival / Raymond Martin.
p.   cm.—(Cambridge studies in philosophy)
Includes bibliographical references and index.
ISBN 0-521-59266-6 (hardbound)
1. Self (Philosophy)   2. Identity (Psychology)   3. Future life.
I. Title.   II. Series.
BD450.M27717   1998
126–dc21   98-22320
                                        CIP

A catalog record for this book is available from the British Library.

ISBN 0 521 59266 6 hardback

To Louis and Ann Martin
my parents

Contents

Preface

Occasionally, but not often, philosophers discover something genuinely new – a new problem or a subtle change in an old problem that brings a new set of issues into focus. When this happens circumstances are ripe for transformations not just of what we believe but also of what we think is worth considering and how we think we ought to proceed.

Beginning in the late 1960s something genuinely new happened in the centuries-old philosophical debate over personal identity; more precisely, something new would have happened, had it not happened once before, in the eighteenth century (this earlier discussion then was forgotten). What was new, on both occasions, is that tacit and extremely natural assumptions about the importance of identity in a person's so-called self-interested concern to survive were called into question. As a consequence, the traditional philosophical focus on metaphysics gave rise to new normative and empirical inquiries about what matters in survival. In these new inquiries fundamental and potentially unsettling questions were raised, for the first time (and *as if* for the first time), about the significance of the distinction between self and other.

The revolutionary and controversial thesis that identity is *not* what matters primarily in survival has been a principal focus of the more recent debate. The version of this idea that has gotten by far the most attention is the normative thesis that identity is *not* what *should* matter primarily in survival. This normative thesis has been endorsed by several influential philosophers. Subsequently, however, other influential philosophers have vigorously defended the traditional idea that identity should matter primarily in survival, or at least that it is a precondition of what should matter primarily. Currently the traditional idea seems to have made a comeback.

In my view, the question of what matters in survival is crucial to philosophical self-understanding and, hence, needs to be discussed. However, I doubt that there is a feasible way of showing either that identity should matter primarily in survival or that it should not matter. I want, then, to try to motivate a shift in the philosophical debate from the normative question of whether this or that should matter in survival to the largely descriptive question of what – that is rationally permissible – actually does or might be brought to matter. In my view, to many people, whose beliefs and values are rationally permissible, identity does not or will not on reflection matter primarily – at least, it will not matter at the familiar theoretical level at which we articulate our beliefs. However, it is not crucial to what I mainly want to say that I be right about this. For one thing, in addition to this theoretical level of belief, which is the only level that so far has been discussed in the debate over what matters in survival, there is also an experiential level at which beliefs or things that function as if they were beliefs make their presence felt; and, in my view, these experiential beliefs, or quasi-beliefs, throw into doubt virtually all of the conclusions about what matters in survival that have been advanced based just on a consideration of theoretical beliefs. For another, I do not intend to defend *any* thesis about what matters in survival but, rather, to provide a rationale and a model for a new kind of investigation of our deepest egoistic survival values, the ultimate purpose of which is not merely to discover what our values actually are, but to do that in a way that facilitates their transformation.

Had it not been for Derek Parfit's paper "Personal Identity" (1971), and subsequently his *Reasons and Persons* (1984), I would not have written the present book. Parfit showed me, perhaps without intending that any reader should draw such a lesson from his work, how to connect to the philosophical debate over personal identity what I had taken to be extraphilosophical reflections on the experience of self. Before Parfit's paper appeared I had been relatively uninterested in the analytic personal identity debate because of its preoccupation with what I regarded as trivial questions of conceptual analysis and because of its neglect of experience. Parfit showed me (and everyone else) how to make the transition from that traditional debate to the question of what matters in survival. He did this by taking the focus off of language (and conceptual analysis) and putting it squarely on questions about our deepest so-called egoistic values. It seemed (and still does seem) to me that it is but a short step from these values to experience. In the present book I take that step.

I have also learned a great deal from the writings and in some cases the patient criticism of several other personal identity theorists, particularly Sydney Shoemaker, Robert Nozick, John Perry, Peter Unger, Ernest Sosa, Stephen White, and Ingmar Persson. To varying degrees, their influence resonates throughout the present book.

Several of the chapters that follow are developments and revisions of ideas I've published elsewhere (see References). I want, once again, to thank those who, through their comments or criticisms, helped with these earlier papers. These include: Michael Slote, Brian Garrett, Ernest Sosa, Peter Unger, Jerry Levinson, Richard Wollheim, Susan Wolf, Kadri Vihvelin, R. M. Hare, Denis Robinson, James Baillie, Stiv Fleishman, Daniel Kolak, Xiao-Guang Wang, Richmond Campbell, Sue Sherman, Duncan MacIntosh, Terry Tomkow, Nathan Brett, Steven Braude, Lydia Goehr, Robert Martin, Melinda Hogan, John Biro, Timothy Cleveland, Paul Sagal, Tara Brach, Tom Eigelsbach, Thomas W. Clark, Richard Hanley, and John Barresi.

In many cases what I've used from these earlier papers has been so substantially reworked for the present book that it is difficult now even for me to trace the connections. Still, there is a unity of purpose throughout these papers and this book. In the papers I was trying, not always successfully, to clear a philosophical space for the examination of certain issues having to do with the phenomenology of our most basic egoistic survival values. In this book, I've tried to explore these issues largely from the perspective of that space.

Many people have commented perceptively on earlier drafts of all or part of the present book. Over a period of six years John Barresi has shared with me his reactions to several incarnations of each of the chapters. His patient and perceptive criticisms and encouragement resulted in many improvements. Ingmar Persson, over a period of three years, went through several late versions of this book and made extensive written comments, as well as met with me for three days to talk about the question of what matters in survival. Although he may not accept some of my central claims and arguments, his detailed and insightful comments have led me to revise both in important ways. Thomas W. Clark, Kenneth Feigenbaum, and Paul Torek also each went through an entire late draft of the book and provided me with many helpful comments. I'm very grateful to each of these friends and also to many others, particularly to students who have attended my seminars over the years and who have helped and are unmentioned. In addition to these debts, in the Introduction and in the final chapter, I draw on work published originally in two papers, one of which I wrote jointly with John Barresi (1995) and the other with John and Alessandro Giovannelli (forthcoming). I am very grateful to John and Alessandro for allowing me to draw on this work we did together.

Finally, I thank everyone at Cambridge University Press who worked on this book for being so exceptionally competent and helpful, in particular, my copy editor, Robert Racine, my production editor, Edith Feinstein, and my executive editor, Terence Moore.

Introduction

From Plato until John Locke personal identity was explained in the West primarily by appeal to the notion of a spiritual substance or soul. From Locke until the late 1960s it was explained both in this Platonic way and by appeal to physical and/or psychological relations between a person at one time and one at another (and theorists assumed that how earlier and later persons are related to each other, through intervening persons, by itself determines whether the two are the same person). Since the 1960s there have been three major developments: First, so-called intrinsic relational views have been largely superseded by extrinsic relational (or closest-continuer, or externalist) views, according to which what determines whether a person at one time and one at another are identical is not just how the two are related to each other but also how they are related to every other person. Second, the traditional metaphysical debate over personal identity has spawned a closely related but relatively novel debate over egoistic survival values. This debate has been over the question of whether – from what in actual, as opposed to hypothetical, circumstances would pass for a self-interested point of view – identity or other relations that do not suffice for identity do and/or should matter primarily in survival. And, third, some theorists have replaced the traditional three-dimensional view of persons with a four-dimensional view, according to which the relata of the identity relation are not (whole) persons at short intervals of time but, rather, appropriately unified aggregates of person-stages that collectively span a lifetime.

Two of these developments seem to be here to stay. Extrinsic relational views, while somewhat controversial, have largely replaced the older intrinsic relational views. And the four-dimensional view, while it hasn't replaced the three-dimensional view, is widely accepted, even by those who prefer a three-dimensional view, as an alternative way to understand persons. The fate of the remaining third-phase development, which hinges on that of the revolutionary thesis that identity is *not* what matters primarily in survival, still hangs in the balance. Although this thesis was endorsed initially by Shoemaker (1970) and Parfit (1971) (and later by Nozick, 1981), subsequently, several other influential philosophers, including Lewis (1976,1983), Sosa (1990), and Unger (1991), have argued forcefully for the traditional idea that identity *is* (or is a precondition of) what matters primarily in survival (henceforth, understand the expression *what matters in survival* to include the qualification, *or is a precondition of what matters*). Still other philosophers (e.g., Wilkes, 1988; Donagan, 1990; and Baillie, 1993) have questioned the philosophical significance of hypothetical examples of (possibly) impossible situations, on which the whole debate over what matters primarily in survival depends.

More than anything else, it has been fission examples that are responsible for the recent revolution in personal identity theory. In the sort of fission examples that have been most discussed, a person somehow divides – in David Wiggins's initial illustrations, amoeba-like – into two or more (seemingly) numerically different persons, each of whom initially is qualitatively identical to the other(s) and also to the prefission person from whom they both (all) emerged (Wiggins,1967). (That is how on a three-dimensional view of persons one would describe what happens; in Chapters 4 and 5 I explain how it would be described on a four-dimensional view and also why for the issues that concern me it does not matter which view I adopt.) The consideration of fission examples motivated philosophers to face the possibility that people might be continued by others whose existences they would value as much as their own and in pretty much the same ways as they would value their own. It also motivated philosophers, appropriately enough, to separate two questions that they had been treating as one: the traditional question of determining what are the necessary and sufficient conditions for personal identity over time and the new question of determining what matters primarily in survival.

The fission examples that in recent times have preoccupied philosophers are for the most part science-fiction scenarios far removed from the practical realities of day-to-day life and death. But these examples have been inspired by real life situations. In the late 1930s, neurosurgeons in the United States began performing a procedure in which they severed the corpus callosums of severe epileptics in the hope of confining their seizures to one hemisphere of their brains and thus reducing their severity. Often this procedure was doubly successful in that it reduced not only the severity of the seizures but also their frequency. However, it also had a bizarre side-effect, not discovered until many years later. It seemingly created two independent centers of consciousness within the same human skull. These

2

apparent centers of consciousness lacked introspective access to each other; they could be made to acquire and express information independently of each other; and, most dramatically, they sometimes differed volitionally, expressing their differences using alternate sides of the same human bodies they jointly shared. In one case, a man who had had this operation reportedly hugged his wife with one arm while he pushed her away with the other; in another a man tried with his right hand (controlled by his left, verbal hemisphere) to hold a newspaper where he could read it, thereby blocking his view of the TV, while he tried with his left hand (controlled by his right hemisphere) to knock the paper out of the way.

The fission examples of philosophers are tidier and more complete than these real life cases. As a result they have brought the issue of egoistic survival values into sharper theoretical focus. However, their use in connection with the debate over personal identity and related issues has become controversial. In particular some have argued that because these fission examples are of (possibly) impossible situations, the consideration of them cannot shed any light on what matters in survival. I shall return to these worries in Chapter 1. First, though, it is worth recognizing that fission examples are not merely a by-product of the recent consideration of science-fiction scenarios. Rather, consideration of them had arisen previously in the eighteenth century (for a fuller account than the one about to be given, see Martin and Barresi, 1995; Martin, Barresi, and Giovannelli, forthcoming).

With the exception of Spinoza, Western theorists of personal identity prior to John Locke took the identity of people to depend essentially on the continuity of their souls. Their view was that souls were immaterial, indivisible, and hence naturally immortal. They argued about how matter could combine with souls to form living persons. But since almost all of the theorists who were party to this debate were Christians, they accepted, and were concerned to provide an account that would explain, how the same people who had lived on Earth could live again in the afterlife. They agreed that the persistence of souls would underwrite everyone's persistence into the afterlife, but they hotly debated whether, once there, the soul would rejoin with matter that formed the person's body on Earth or, instead, would join with a body made of different matter.

Locke's innovation was the genuinely radical and progressive thesis that the identities of resurrected people do not depend on their having either the same souls or the same bodies, or even the same matter, but, rather, on their having the same consciousnesses. In supporting this explosive new idea Locke was preoccupied with the implications of fissionlike examples, such as his "day-man/night-man" example (1694/1975, II, ch. 27, sec. 23). Most of his fissionlike examples do not involve one consciousness dividing into two, each of which is then continuous with the original, contemporaneous with the other, and yet independent of the other. Hence, most are not genuine fission examples. However, Locke eventually goes on to consider the possibility that in a case in which one's little finger is cut off, consciousness might not only stay with the main part of the body or only go with the little finger, but instead might split and go with both: "Though if the same Body should still live, and immediately from the separation of the little Finger have its own peculiar consciousness, whereof the little Finger knew nothing, it would not at all be concerned for it, as a part of it *self,* or could own any of its Actions, or have any of them imputed to him" (1694/1975, II, 27, 18). In giving this example Locke became the first personal identity theorist to consider a genuine fission example explicitly. And although he did not then go on to explore its implications for his theory of personal identity, once he published his new theory the fission example cat was out of the bag.

Locke also introduced several distinctions that are crucial to considering fission examples and that have figured importantly in the post-1960s discussion. For instance, when he said, "For as to this point of being the same *self,* it matters not whether this present *self* be made up of the same or other Substances; I being as much concern'd and as justly accountable for any Action was done a thousand Years since, appropriated to me now by this self-consciousness, as I am, for what I did the last moment" (1694/1975, II, 27, 16), he linked the question of whether a person persists to that of whether a present self-consciousness has a special kind (or degree) of *concern* for someone in the past and is *accountable* for and has *appropriated* the actions of someone in the past. It is a short step from the separation of these three elements that ordinarily attend personal persistence to considering the possibility that one or more of these elements might obtain even when a person does not persist.

Whatever his own intentions may have been, Locke also suggested, to both critics and admirers of his new theory, that people are fictional entities. In the first edition of the *Essay* he did this by the uses to which he put his distinction between the "natural" and the "moral" man. In subsequent editions he did it by distinguishing between man as an *animal,* whose nature presumably it is the job of science to discover, and man as a *rational being,* that is, a *person,* which Locke seems to have regarded as a normatively defined hybrid. Although the details are complicated, Locke at the least seems to have been working toward the view, and may even have arrived at it, that persons come into being as a natural by-product of processes of identification and the application of self-concepts that are ingredients in reflexive consciousness (see, e.g., Law, 1823, III, pp. 177–201; Behan, 1979; Ayers, 1991, II, pp. 273–7).

From 1706 to 1709 Locke's fissionlike examples and his suggestions leaning toward the view that persons are fictions had a remarkable development in the six-part published debate between Samuel Clarke and Anthony Collins. In this exchange Clarke defended a traditional, spiritual substance view of self and Collins a view very like Locke's (Clarke, 1738/1928, III, pp. 720–913). Ironically, from our current perspective, it was Clarke, rather than Collins, who introduced the idea of fission. He introduced it in order to make the point that a sequence of like consciousnesses is not the same as a series of acts by a single consciousness:

> Such a Consciousness in a Man, whose Substance is wholly changed, can no more make it Just and Equitable for such a Man to be punished for an Action done by another Substance; than the Addition of the like Consciousness (by the Power of God) to two or more new created Men; or to any Number of Men now living, by giving a like Modification to the Motion of the Spirits in the Brain of each of them respectively, could make them All to be one and the same individual Person, at the same time that they remain several and distinct Persons; or make it just and reasonable for all and every one of them to be punished for one and the same individual Action, done by one only, or perhaps by none of them at all. (pp. 844–5)

In this imaginary fission scenario Clarke thought Collins's view would lead him to having to say of two or more individuals that they are and also are not the same persons. Clarke subsequently reiterated several variations on this example. Although the debate between Clarke and Collins is not often discussed explicitly by subsequent eighteenth-century philosophers, there are many indications that it was widely read. These, then, are evidence that philosophers generally were at least aware of fission examples.

We know that Joseph Butler was familiar with the debate between Clarke and Collins, even though he never discusses it, because he twice footnotes it (1736/1852, pp. 32, 321). However, Butler does discuss some of the key themes that emerged in the debate. His best known thought on personal identity is, of course, his charge that the memory analysis of it is circular. However, immediately after making this famous objection to the memory view, he highlights two other issues that had surfaced both in Locke and in the Clarke–Collins debate. The issues are, first, that there are certain important links among identity, responsibility, and self-concern and, second, that on a view such as Locke's it is questionable whether persons (or selves) are real or merely fictional.

Butler introduced these issues by asking "whether the same rational being is the same substance," which, he said, "needs no answer because Being and Substance, in this place, stand for the same idea" (1736/1852, p. 320). He continued, "The consciousness of our own existence, in youth and in old age, or in any two joint successive moments, is not the *same individual action,* i.e., not the same consciousness, but different successive consciousnesses" (pp. 320–1). And, yet, "the person, of whose existence the consciousness is felt now, and was felt an hour or a year ago, is discerned to be, not two persons, but one and the same person; and therefore is one and the same" (p. 321). From this, he said, "It must follow" on a view such as Locke's, that,

> it is a fallacy upon ourselves to charge our present selves with any thing we did, or to imagine our present selves interested in any thing which befell us yesterday; or that our present self will be interested in what will befall us tomorrow; since our present self is not, in reality, the same with the self of yesterday, but another like self or person coming in its room, and mistaken for it; to which another self will succeed tomorrow. This, I say, must follow: for if the self or person of today, and that of tomorrow, are not the same, but only like persons the person of today is really no more interested in what will befall the person of tomorrow than in what will befall any other person. (p. 322)

Butler conceded that "those who maintain" the view he is criticizing "allow that a person is the same as far back as his remembrance reaches" and "use the *words, identity* and *same* person" (p. 322). And, he pointed out, "Language [will not] permit these words to be laid aside, since if they were, there must be I know not what ridiculous periphrasis substituted in the room of them" (p. 322). But, he claimed, Lockeans "cannot, consistently with themselves, mean, that the person is really the same . . . but only that he is so in a *fictitious* sense: in such a sense only as they assert, for this they do assert, that *any number of persons whatever may be the same person*" (p. 322; emphasis added). Butler concluded that a person or self "is not an idea, or abstract notion, or quality, but a being only, which is capable of life and action, of happiness and misery," and, hence, not a fiction (p. 323).

In sum, so far as Butler was concerned, if Locke's view were true, our present selves would have no reason to be especially concerned about our future selves or to hold themselves accountable for what our past selves had done. Yet, in Butler's view, regardless of our philosophical views we must retain the language of self and person. So, if Locke's view were true, even though we would continue to speak of selves and persons in a normal way, we would have to consider there to be selves and persons only in a fictitious sense. Butler thought that this refuted Locke's view, but not because he thought he could prove Locke's view is false (he admitted he could not; 1736/1852, p. 325). Rather, he thought it refuted Locke's view because "the bare unfolding this notion [that selves are merely fictitious entities] and laying it thus naked and open, seems the best confutation of it" (p. 322).

Neither David Hume nor Adam Smith ever discussed the question of personal identity in anything like the way in which Locke, Clarke, Collins, or Butler discussed it; for instance, neither had anything to say that is directly relevant to the question of which relations are crucial to personal persistence. Perhaps as a consequence neither Hume nor Smith discussed fission examples. Thomas Reid, though, may have commented on fission examples, albeit briefly, when he said of Locke's view of personal identity that it "hath some strange consequences, which the author was aware of, Such as, that, if the same consciousness can be transferred from one intelligent being to another, which he thinks we cannot shew to be impossible, then two or twenty intelligent beings may be the same person" (Reid, 1785, VI, p. 3). However, there is no way to tell exactly what Reid had in mind. Others, such as Abraham Tucker, also discussed fission examples (1763/1984, pp. 204–5; 1768–77/1977, pp. 73, 80–1). But so far as the question of what matters in survival is concerned, the real breakthroughs came in the writings of Joseph Priestley and William Hazlitt, to whom I shall return in Chapter 6. For now, the important point is that concern with the question of what matters in survival is not a by-product of recently concocted science-fiction-generated fission examples, but, rather, a recurring theme in the history of modern philosophy. Moreover it is a theme that has struck to the roots of peoples' existential involvement with their views of their own natures and prospects.

A puzzle remains. Since fission examples were discussed throughout the eighteenth (and even into the nineteenth) century, why didn't the same sort of theoretical revolution that has occurred in our own times occur then, at least in the work of those who were sympathetic to a relational account of identity? In other words, why, in the eighteenth century, didn't the ideas that precipitated the revolution in personal identity theory in our own times ever really catch on?

Somewhat surprisingly, from our current perspective, part of the answer has to be that there were not many influential eighteenth-century

7

theorists who were sympathetic to relational accounts of personal identity. Locke and Hume were sympathetic, but Hume chose not to discuss the kinds of examples that might have led him to anticipate post-1960s developments. Collins was sympathetic, but he was not an important philosopher and may even have set the cause back by allowing himself to be upstaged by Clarke. Berkeley, Butler, Reid, and Tucker were substance theorists. As we shall see, Priestley and Hazlitt were sympathetic, but Priestley did not discuss personal identity and survival all that much, and Hazlitt had the misfortune of writing just before Kant burst onto the scene and changed the topic.

The revolution in personal identity theory that has occurred in our own times required that thinkers go beyond the relational view of personal identity. But before thinkers could go beyond that view they first had to accept it. And surprising as it may sound to us today, the relational view wasn't generally accepted in the eighteenth century. In fact, it wasn't even *generally* accepted in the nineteenth (see, e.g., how Sidgwick uses the substance view to deflect worries about what matters in survival; 1907/1874, p. 418). For its general acceptance the relational view had to await the twentieth century, by which time Priestley and Hazlitt were rarely read by personal identity theorists, and fission examples, despite the brief mention of them in Locke and Reid, had been largely forgotten.

Another part of the answer is that, in the eighteenth century, fission examples tended to be introduced into the debate over personal identity not as a way of developing a relational view, but rather as an *objection* to it. Those, like Collins, who were sympathetic to Locke, were intent on defending a Lockean view against a threatened retreat back into what they regarded as obscurantist metaphysics. They saw fission examples as a possible motivation for such a retreat. So, the context was not conducive to anyone's seeing that fission examples, rather than an objection to a relational approach, were a way of pushing that approach to even more radical conclusions.

Finally, in spite of the widespread misconception that, during the Enlightenment, religious dogma beat a hasty retreat before the mighty advance of secular rationality, Christianity, in particular, even among the best thinkers of the age, held its ground (indeed, it is still somewhat holding its ground). Before thinkers generally could seriously question the importance of personal identity, the influence of Christianity had to be blunted. From the eighteenth to the twentieth centuries most important Western thinkers who took self and personal identity theory seriously were Christians. As such, they accepted the idea that there will be a resurrection attended by divine rewards and punishments. Few had Priestley's ability, or even his motivation, to envision how those rewards and punishments might on a relational view, let alone in the absence of personal persistence, still serve the cause of divine justice and human morality. And, even in our own times, well-regarded philosophers have expressed doubts about whether in the absence of personal persistence a version of resurrection acceptable to Christians can be worked out (Ayers, 1991, II, p. 272).

1

Questions

In our own times the use of hypothetical examples in connection with the debate over personal identity and related issues has become controversial. In particular, some have argued that because these examples are of (possibly) impossible situations, the consideration of them cannot shed light on what matters in survival. Since in the present study I intend to make use of hypothetical examples of (possibly) impossible situations, I want now to defend the uses to which I shall put them. To do that, I first specify a fission example that is a modified version of one originally presented by Shoemaker (1984, p. 119). Then I use this example to explain why fission examples, in particular, and hypothetical examples of (possibly) impossible situations, in general, are not only a legitimate but perhaps an indispensable tool in revealing what matters to people in survival.

Imagine, then, that you have a health problem that will result soon in your sudden and painless death unless you receive one or the other of two available treatments. The first is to have your brain removed and placed into the empty cranium of a body that, except for being brainless, is qualitatively identical to your own. The second is to have your brain removed, divided into functionally identical halves (each capable of sustaining your full psychology), and then to have each of these halves put into the empty cranium of a body of its own, again one that is brainless but otherwise qualitatively identical to your own.

In the first treatment there is a 10 percent chance that the transplantation will take. If it takes, the survivor who wakes up in the recovery room will be physically and psychologically like you just prior to the operation except that he will know he has had the operation and will be healthy. In the second there is a 95 percent chance that both transplantations will take. If both take, each of the survivors who wakes up in the recovery room will be physically and psychologically like you just prior to the operation except that each of them will know he has had the operation and each will be healthy. If the transplantation in the first treatment does not take, the would-be survivor will die painlessly on the operating table. If either transplantation in the second treatment does not take, the other will not take either, and both would-be survivors will die painlessly on the operating table. Everything else about the treatments – suppose – is the same and as attractive to you as possible: For instance, both treatments are painless, free of charge, and, if successful, result in survivors who recover quickly.

Many philosophers believe that identity would be retained in the first (nonfission) treatment but lost in the second (fission) treatment. They think that identity would be lost in the second treatment because they believe, first, that identity is a transitive relationship – which implies that if one of the survivors were the same person as the brain donor, and the donor were the same person as the other survivor, then the former survivor would be the same person as the latter survivor; second, that the survivors, at least once they began to lead independent lives, are not plausibly regarded as the same people as each other; and, third, that it would be arbitrary to regard just one of the survivors but not the other as the same person as the donor (at the moment the survivors originate, they are equally qualified). Hence, in the view of these philosophers, it is more plausible to regard each of the survivors as a different person from the donor.

Assume, for the sake of argument, that this way of viewing what will happen in the two treatments is correct. On this assumption, you would persist through the first treatment but not the second. So, given the circumstances specified in the example, only by sacrificing your identity could you greatly increase the chances of someone who initially would be qualitatively just like you surviving for years. The question is whether in the circumstances specified it would be worth it for you to have such an operation, that is, whether it would be worth it for what in more normal circumstances would be considered as selfish (or self-regarding) reasons. Many who consider examples like this one feel strongly that it would be worth it. So, for them, at least, it would seem that ceasing and being continued by others can matter as much, or almost as much, as surviving. I shall call the reasoning (just sketched) that is thought to support this conclusion the "fission argument."

QUESTIONABLE ASSUMPTIONS

The fission argument depends on the questionable assumptions, first, that identity is a transitive relationship; second, that the donor in a fission procedure is just one person; and, third, that some people, if they were to project themselves into the position of the person facing the choice situation depicted in the example and were to choose rationally and solely for egoistic or self-regarding reasons, could choose the second treatment over the first.

The assumption that identity is transitive is so well entrenched in the ways we think about it that a persuasive argument that it should not be regarded as transitive would have to include a specification of the circumstances under which we are and are not entitled to infer from X is identical to Y, and Y to Z, that X is identical to Z (see, e.g., Perry, 1972). So far no such specification has attracted much support.

Regarding the second of the assumptions, David Lewis has claimed that the donor in a fission procedure is not a person but, rather, a person-stage (roughly, a time slice of a person). Persons, on Lewis's four-dimensional view, are aggregates of person-stages that in normal circumstances collectively span what ordinarily we would regard as an entire human lifetime. In unusual circumstances, such as when there has been fission, persons share some of their stages with other persons. What in the fission argument is called the "donor" is, in Lewis's view, actually a shared prefission person-stage of at least two persons, each of whom includes (among other person-stages) one or the other (but not both) of the two postfission person-stages that emerge simultaneously immediately after the operation. In this view, so long as in the fission procedure sufficient psychological continuity has been preserved, there is no loss or gain of personal identity; that is, since the people who will eventually separate initially overlap, fission does not cause new people to begin to exist but merely makes it apparent that the so-called donor was a person-stage of more than one person. Thus, Lewis's way of objecting to the fission argument does not depend on questioning whether identity is transitive but, rather, denies that the fission operation separates identity from other characteristics that might then be said to matter more in survival than identity.

The third debatable assumption underlying the fission argument is that some people, if they were to project themselves into the position of the person facing the choice situation depicted in the example and were to choose rationally and solely for egoistic or self-regarding reasons, could choose the second treatment over the first; that is, that a prefission person's choice to cease and be continued by others, when he may have a way of surviving that is much better than death, could be both rational and egoistic (or self-regarding). In ensuing chapters, I explain how such a choice could be both rational and "egoistic." I also think (and shall assume in my discussion) that many people actually would choose the second

12

treatment. However, my argument about the importance of identity in survival will not depend on my being right that many people would chose the second treatment. Nor will it depend on the outcome of the debate over either of the first two assumptions.

METHODOLOGY

Hypothetical thought experiments of (possibly) impossible situations have been a mainstay of the personal identity literature since Locke's *Essay* and of philosophy generally since Plato's *Republic* (Gyges's ring). Even so, their use in connection with the discussion of personal identity and egoistic survival values has been challenged. According to Kathleen Wilkes, in a passage that captures the heart of this challenge, "We can rule out absolutely the fission or fusion of humans," neither of which is "theoretically possible"; the thought experimenter, she says, who "plays" with these notions "has crossed the tenuous and amorphous line between philosophy and fairy story, and his play is not philosophy; for the original, and originally worrying, question was what we would say if *we* divided or fused" (1988, p. 37; see also Donagan, 1990). It follows, in this view, that if we cannot divide, what we should say about people who can divide has no evidential value either for theories of personal identity or in assessing what matters to us in survival.

I claim that whatever the merit of Wilkes's point in connection with the debate over personal identity, it has none whatsoever in connection with that over what matters in survival. To see why her point is without merit, it is necessary to separate the basis for her prohibition against fission examples from other (more) local worries that philosophers have expressed. One of these local worries, as we have seen, is whether fission would indeed undermine personal identity, something that may be doubted either from the standpoint of a four-dimensional view of persons or from that of questioning the transitivity of identity. Another local worry is whether a person's narrowly self-interested choice to fission could be rational.

Such local worries are not based on fission examples being of (possibly) impossible situations but on other aspects of them. Wilkes's view, by contrast, is that even if fission were to undermine identity and even if many people, for narrowly self-interested reasons, could and would rationally choose to undergo fission, the choices of these people would be irrelevant to how we should assess the relative importance of personal identity compared with other of our egoistic survival values. The reason, it seems, that Wilkes is so sure about this is that fission examples tend to depend for their evidential value on our being able to project ourselves into the positions of the choosers in them and she thinks that to so project ourselves we would have to suppose we are different than we actually are.

In my view, if this worry of Wilkes is to have any force, her point would have to be that to project ourselves into the positions of the choosers in these examples, we would have to suppose not only that we are different than we are, but also that we are different in ways that block inferences back to our current values. There, as we shall see, is the rub. The fact that a choice situation is impossible does not imply that we cannot use our beliefs about what choices we would make in it as evidence about our values. A fission example can expose what we would choose if we were just like we actually are except for differences that would not affect our values but, rather, simply afford us options we do not now have. So long as our psychologies as choosers in these examples, including our desires, motives, beliefs, intentions, and values, are just what they actually are and so long as we psychologically process whatever affects us – except possibly for our processing it redundantly – just like we would process it in ordinary circumstances, then whether we would choose fission over other options, if we had such a choice, can be psychologically revealing.

Even if we assume, for the sake of argument, that in principle our brains cannot be split into functionally identical halves, each capable of sustaining our full psychologies, still we can imagine people who are just like us except that their brains can be so split, and split in ways that never cause them to decide differently than we would decide if we were faced with their options. Indeed, we can imagine that we are such people. Under these circumstances what we would choose, if we were in the positions that the imaginary choosers in these examples are in, is obviously relevant to determining what we value. For the assumption that we are such people does not require us to suppose that our values or how we process and express them are any different, except for their being redundantly encoded in our brains, than they actually are. And redundant encoding is not a kind of difference that would block inferences from the choices we would make in such hypothetical circumstances back to our actual values.

One might object that people in a society in which fission were an option would *have to be* different from us since the science and/or technology of such a society would have to be more advanced than our own (Wilkes, 1988, p. 11; Baillie, 1993, pp. 82ff). Not so. Even if it were true that people in such a society generally would be different, it would not follow that everybody in such a society would have to have a psychology and/or background information different from people now. After all, not everyone even in our own society knows about the latest developments in science and technology. For the purposes of the kinds of arguments under consideration, all we have to imagine is that there might be one person in such a society whose psychology and background information are relevantly similar to our own. Surely it is possible, even in such an advanced society, that there would be one such person.

For such reasons Wilkes's criticism of the use of fission examples provides no basis whatsoever for doubting whether examples of (possibly) impossible situations, and in particular of fission, can shed light on what matters in survival. There are legitimate methodological worries about the uses to which fission examples and other hypothetical examples may be put. We shall deal with these worries as they arise. None of them of which I am aware motivates a general prohibition against the use of hypothetical examples of (possibly) impossible situations.

ALTERNATIVE APPROACHES TO THE QUESTION OF WHAT MATTERS

Ironically, the philosophical debate over what matters in survival has tended to be over the normative question of whether and, if so, how much identity ought rationally to matter. The revolutionaries, led by Parfit, have argued that however much identity may actually matter, it ought not to matter primarily. The traditionalists have argued that identity ought to matter primarily. In my view, this preoccupation with the question of whether identity ought or ought not to matter is a mistake. There is not any feasible way for theorists on either side to make out their respective cases. And the reason for that is that among sophisticated naturalistically inclined philosophers, disagreements over the importance of identity as a so-called egoistic survival value tend to depend not on cognitive error but, rather, on differences in temperament. The most salient of these differences tends to get expressed in the differing responses philosophers make to the question of how much it should matter that a distinction depends merely on conventional or linguistic considerations. Typically those who are disposed to argue that identity should not matter primarily have assumed that merely conventional considerations ought not to impinge importantly on our values, which, they say, ought to be brought more closely into harmony with the way the world actually is. Those who have argued that identity should matter primarily have tended to assume that in the case of identity some merely conventional considerations ought to impinge importantly on our values. A central question for both groups of philosophers, then, is whether there is any way to show how much merely conventional considerations ought to matter. In my view, there is not.

Suppose, for instance, that with the possible exception of personal identity it were never the case that merely conventional considerations ought to matter. Then, the revolutionaries could draw on that fact to argue that merely conventional considerations ought not to matter when it comes to identity either. But the supposition is not true. In games, merely conventional considerations matter a great deal. And in games the fact that merely conventional considerations matter a great deal does not seem always to be due to something else's mattering that is not merely conventional. For instance, someone might suggest that the conventions in a game matter only because of our commitment to some such moral rule as: Once a game has begun it is not fair to change the rules. But imagine someone playing golf alone; even though she could change the rules from the normal ones without being unfair to anyone, still playing by the normal rules might be important to her, for any number of reasons. She may want to compare her score with previous scores when she or others played by the normal rules; or she may want to know how well she can do at *golf* rather than at some game of her own invention; and so on. In general, it is implausible to suppose that our commitment to some moral rule, such as the one mentioned that pertains to fairness, is what gives conventions in games whatever importance they might have. And because other proposals of which I am aware fare no better, it seems simpler just to concede that conventions in games can be important in their own right. Nor is the importance of merely conventional considerations restricted to games. In other areas of our lives also, such as those having to do with making money or acknowledging national borders, merely conventional considerations seem to matter a great deal.

An additional problem for those who would argue that when it comes to personal identity, merely conventional considerations should not matter is that of explaining how to draw the line between merely conventional considerations and other sorts of considerations. Suppose, for instance, that June is keenly aware that due to her lack of experience she is naive when it comes to matters of the heart. She wonders whether the complicated feelings she has for her therapist constitute "true love." Her friend, Alice, informs her that her feelings may be a transference phenomenon of a sort that frequently occurs in therapy. Alice tells June that feelings like hers are often mistaken by patients for true love and advises her to be cautious about taking these feelings too seriously and/or acting on them. Under these circumstances June might reasonably regard it as important to read up on transference phenomena before acting on her feelings. And in consulting the professional literature, she might not only learn about the range of emotional possibilities available to her, but also come to regard it as important that she discover the correct classification for her feelings, so that she can learn where she stands with respect to this range of possibilities.

In circumstances such as those in which June finds herself, is the difference between true love and transference phenomenon real or merely conventional? Before answering, change the example slightly. Suppose that June, instead of going weekly to a professional therapist, has recently acquired a friend, George, with whom she gets together once a week over coffee. George is a nice guy and a good listener. He takes a sympathetic interest in June's problems and is always patient and nonjudgmental. When June talks to him about things that are troubling her, mostly he just listens. Understandably June likes this about him. Soon she finds that she is confiding in him. On these occasions George often says things that help draw June out. Occasionally he also suggests for her consideration interpretations that she might be able to use to make emotional sense out of her life. After several such meetings June discovers that her feelings for George have gone beyond friendship. Keenly aware that she is naive when it comes to matters of the heart, she wonders whether her feelings for George constitute "true love?" She talks it over with Alice, who tells her, . . . tells her what? What would you tell June if you were Alice?

Issues like the ones in these examples can be vitally important to people. And reasonably so. In a real case that is like the first of these examples, a woman in June's position, without talking it over with anyone and without knowing much about the dynamics of psychotherapy, decided she was in love with her therapist and proceeded to have an affair with him. Later she learned that her feelings would be regarded by many therapists as a transference phenomenon of a sort that often occurs in therapy. She thereby also realized that her therapist/lover must have known this all along and yet not told her. She felt betrayed and humiliated. Had she known in advance, she insisted, she would not have had the affair, or at least she would not have entered into it so quickly. She considered suing her therapist.

A basic problem, then, for the philosopher who would say that when it comes to the value of personal identity, merely conventional considerations should not matter all that much is that in so much of life they matter a great deal. Another basic problem is that it is difficult to say what counts as a merely conventional consideration. A third problem is that – worries about conventional considerations aside – it is difficult, *in general,* to put any but the mildest limits, based mostly on considerations of coherence, on what rationally can matter to a person. This is largely because it is easy to develop contexts in which the seemingly most irrelevant things can matter rationally.

Consider, for instance, how you might come to care more about an experience if it happened to you while you were wearing a red shirt than if it happened while you were wearing a shirt of some other color. Suppose that many of the most positive events in your life – the births of your children, your winning of the lottery, and so on – happened while you were wearing a red shirt. You were unaware of this at the time. Much later, looking at old photographs, you noticed it. Subsequently you also noticed that, apparently by chance, the pattern continued. Soon you developed a special feeling about red shirts, not because you thought your shirt having been red played a causal role in bringing about significant events in your past, but just because your shirt having been red was associated with them. Now you like the fact that for you red is not just another color but special. Your liking this makes your wearing of a shirt that's red more meaningful (and pleasurable) to you than it would be otherwise. You decide to try to make the red-shirt pattern continue. After making this decision you learn that your long lost lover is returning from abroad. You will meet her at the airport. What color shirt will you wear?

Although the red-shirt example may be far-fetched, it illustrates a problem that is pervasive for those who want to put constraints on what rationally can matter in survival. The problem is that often it is possible to invent a context in which a person who has a worldview more or less like the one the rest of us have, and who has no relevant false beliefs, is especially and rationally concerned about something. The question, then, is whether it is also often possible to invent such a context for such a person's being especially and rationally concerned about his own identity. I argue later that often it is possible. For the moment it is enough to point out that, prima facie, such a context might consist simply in the fact that in modern times virtually everyone, at least (but surely not only) in industrialized countries, has assigned great significance to merely conventional considerations regarding personal identity. It is difficult to show that values that have been so pervasive are *necessarily* irrational.

For such reasons, it seems to me that within broad limits, governed mainly by considerations of coherence among a person's values, there is not going to be a feasible way to show in general how much merely conventional considerations may rationally influence a person's values, at least when it comes to the question of identity. If I am right about that, then there is bound to be a philosophical impasse among those who have radically conflicting views about how much identity ought to matter in survival. The result will be that no one will be able to show that her view is correct. And the reason for this result, it seems, will be that none of the views is correct. Thus, so long as philosophers focus on the normative question of how much identity rationally ought to matter in survival, a philosophical impasse is predictable, and one that may well be irresolvable. Partly for this reason it seems to me that a better philosophical focus than the normative one of trying to determine what ought to matter in survival is the largely descriptive question of what that is rationally permissible actually does matter and, in particular, of whether (and if so, how and how much) identity actually matters. Suitably clarified versions of this descriptive question at least have answers.

I want to suggest as well that an even more worthwhile philosophical focus is that of providing a kind of clarification about our most basic so-called egoistic survival values that can motivate their transformation. This can begin by each person's finding a way that facilitates progressive change to discover what does in fact matter to him in survival. In this more dynamic philosophical/therapeutic program, the ultimate objective would not be to hit a static target – to discover some deep normative or factual truth – but, rather, to set in motion a progressive process the predictable result of which, in the case of many people, will be that identity becomes for them a less important value than it was at the beginning of the inquiry. The process that leads to this result is progressive partly because it is fueled by enhanced clarification. Whether the likely result, the devaluation of identity, often, or ever, will be a good thing are separate questions. In cases, if there are any, in which the devaluation of identity is a good thing, then that is another reason for regarding the process that leads to it as progressive (more on this in Chapter 5).

In the normative debate over what should matter in survival, the revolutionaries have tended to encourage transformation. In that respect, their projects and mine are the same. However, their projects generally have been to try to cause identity to matter less by proving that it should matter less. Parfit provides the premier example of this approach. From my point of view the basic problem with this approach lies neither in its aiming for transformation nor in the kind of transformation for which it aims but, rather, in the way it tries to bring about that transformation: by arguments that, however theoretically interesting, do not establish their intended conclusions, at least not in competition with the views of sophisticated naturalistically inclined adversaries. Another problem with this approach is that even if the revolutionaries' arguments were to establish their conclusions, it is not clear that such arguments would be particularly effective in bringing about progressive changes in peoples' actual values.

In my view, even though the devaluing of personal identity, except in special cases, is not rationally *required,* it may often be rationally *motivated.* Roughly speaking, the difference between these is that, while changes in one's values or attitudes will be rationally required just if it is irrational not to adopt the changes in values, they will be rationally motivated just if the changes are both rationally permissible and brought about by one's becoming relevantly clearer. Thus, rationally motivated changes that are not also rationally required will be somewhat more, in a certain way, than merely rationally permissible changes; yet, since it might be rational not to adopt the values or attitudes, such changes will be somewhat less, in a certain way, than rationally required ones. What does it mean for someone to become *relevantly* clearer? This: A person becomes relevantly clearer just if she becomes clearer overall about who (or what) she is.

OTHER PROBLEMS WITH THE NORMATIVE APPROACH

Imagine that there is a hypothetical example in which you enter into a transformative process in which it is apparently indeterminate whether the person who emerges from the process is you. Previously you had assumed both that whether you exist is always determinate and that it matters a great deal whether you exist. The example calls these assumptions into question, thus causing cognitive dissonance. The survival-value revolutionary says that you should resolve this dissonance by rejecting both of these assumptions, thereby bringing your beliefs and values into greater conformity with the way the world is. The traditionalist says that you should resist the recommended revision of your values and deal with the dissonance in some other way, thereby holding onto deeply seated beliefs and values you have, as well as theories, say, about ethics or rationality, to which you are committed that presuppose these beliefs and values. Who wins?

No one does. The revolutionaries do not win since there is always going to be more than one rationally *permissible* way for you to resolve the dissonance, one of which is the way the traditionalist says you are rationally *required* to resolve it. The traditionalists do not win since a rationally *permissible* way for you to resolve the dissonance is the way the revolutionaries say you are rationally *required* to resolve it. For this reason arguments that something should or should not matter primarily in survival tend to be *normatively imperialistic.* To illustrate what I mean by this, I want now to consider the overall argumentative strategies of two of the main theorists who have tried to show what should matter primarily in survival: Derek Parfit, who has argued powerfully that identity should not matter primarily, and Peter Unger, who has argued powerfully that identity should matter primarily (or at least that it is a precondition of what should matter primarily). My interest will be to focus on their overall strategies – just "the big picture" – rather than on substantive details. I shall consider details later. My hope is that by sketching now what seems to me to be wrong with the overall strategies of Parfit and of Unger, I can begin to discourage interest in the normative project of trying to show, in general, what should matter in survival.

Parfit's Strategy

Parfit (1971; 1984) has tried to show that only psychological connectedness and/or continuity ought to matter in survival and, hence, that physical continuity ought not to matter. That is, he has tried to show that everyone is rationally obligated to regard psychological connectedness and/or continuity as his dominant egoistic survival value and that it is irrational for people to regard physical continuity as an important part of what matters in survival. If Parfit had shown either of these things, then he would have shown that the normative question of what ought to matter in survival is an important one, for then the normative question would have had a startling answer with sweeping philosophical implications. In my view, he has not shown either of these things.

Parfit has a Socratic view of the relative values of the mind and the body. The mind counts for virtually everything. The body has only instrumental value, and it has that only as the vehicle for psychological continuity (hereafter, to be understood to include connectedness). Although Parfit said that physical continuity "is the least important element in a person's continued existence" he conceded that just as one might for sentimental reasons prefer one's original wedding ring to a new ring that is exactly similar, it might not be irrational to care a little about the physical continuity of one's body. However, he never explained why a little bit of sentimental attachment isn't irrational – perhaps just a little bit irrational – nor why, if it is rationally permissible to be a little sentimental about something as relatively insignificant as a wedding ring, it may not be rationally permissible to be very sentimental about something as relatively significant as one's body.

Apparently, the reason why, in Parfit's view, it is not irrational to be a little sentimental about one's wedding ring is because of the ring's historical properties. Your wedding ring, let's suppose, is intimately associated with events now past that had great positive value in and for your life. If you are like most people who value their wedding rings, you value it not because it helps you to remember significant events, say, your engagement or your wedding (presumably you would remember these anyway), but, rather, because the ring helps you to feel psychologically closer to these events and hence helps you to unify your life emotionally. And if you are like most people who feel good about their marriages, that feeling of closeness is important to you. In other words, the ring is a relic. As such, it has great instrumental value over and above its value as a vehicle for psychological continuity. It has this extra value by enhancing a feeling of closeness that is significant to you. But if a mere wedding ring can have great instrumental value over and above its value as a vehicle for psychological continuity, why not also, and even more so, one's own body? The word *sentimental* has pejorative connotations and so it is best to avoid it. The important question is not whether it might be rationally permissible for one to be very sentimental about one's body but, rather, whether it might be rationally permissible to put a high value on one's body in circumstances where there are two guarantees: that one's current body will be replaced immediately by an exact replica; and that only one replica will exist at a time.

Parfit's answer is that it is irrational in such circumstances to put a high value on one's current body; an exact replica would be as good as the original. So, for instance, in his view, a person who chooses to pay much more to travel to Mars via a conventional space trip rather than an equally reliable and much cheaper teletransporter is irrational. But Parfit's defense of this claim assumes that the only reasons that people could have for preferring their bodies to replicas are their beliefs that their bodies are essential to their identities and, hence, that the replicas would be other people. Parfit argued that this is not a good reason for one to prefer one's body to a replica. Even if he is right about this, his defense of the irrationality charge fails. There is another perfectly good reason that people could have for preferring their bodies to replicas.

In the preceding example, a wedding ring helps one to feel psychologically closer to events now past that had great positive value in and for one's life and, thus, has great instrumental value over and above its value as a vehicle for Parfitian psychological continuity. The ring example is not an exceptional case. It illustrates a general and pervasive value phenomenon:

We tend to prefer originals to replicas. Consider, for instance, your attitude toward important historical artifacts, such as Galileo's telescope; great works of art, such as the *Pieta* of Michelangelo, which is in the Vatican; and highly valued objects in nature, such as sequoia stands in California made up of majestic trees that may be the oldest living things on earth. Would you value replicas, made yesterday, of any of these as much as you would value the originals? Set aside the greater resale and prestige value of the originals. Suppose that no one would know you owned or experienced any of these things except yourself. Just considering how it would affect you personally and directly, would you value the replicas as much as the originals?

People may differ in how they answer this question. I find, when I consider it, that I would value the originals much more, for reasons similar to those that emerged in the ring example. The originals help me to feel psychologically closer to the past in ways that I value. The replicas, if I knew they were replicas, could not do this. Hence, the originals would have a great instrumental value that the replicas would lack, and they would have it for reasons that would have nothing to do with false metaphysics. Similarly in the case of our bodies. To treat our bodies as mere vehicles for Parfitian psychological continuity is to ignore other important instrumental values that our bodies may have. Some may value their bodies solely because they believe their bodies are essential to preserving their identities. Others may value their bodies because their bodies have been and are the vehicle for virtually all that has been significant in their lives. Parfit's arguments do not show that *necessarily* it would be irrational to have the latter pattern of values. Thus, so far as his arguments go, physical continuity can matter, and for perfectly acceptable reasons, even if it is not necessary for identity.

Someone might take the view that what I am calling "replicas" are not really replicas since they duplicate only the original object's current properties and not its historical properties. True replicas, on this view, would also duplicate the object's historical properties. So, for instance, a true replica of Galileo's telescope would not only perfectly replicate the current properties of the original, but would also have all of the historical properties of the original, such as that of having been used by Galileo to view mountains on the moon. But unless this objection is simply the claim that there cannot be true replicas of historical objects, then on any ordinary conception of reality it is incoherent. Galileo used one and only one telescope to view mountains on the moon. That telescope's home is a museum in Milan. A replica cannot be that telescope unless, perhaps, the world can split and run in parallel paths, in a scenario similar to that envisaged in the many-worlds interpretation of quantum mechanics. Barring such exotic possibilities the objection is either incoherent or else it is simply the claim that there cannot be true replicas of historical objects. If the objection is the latter claim, then I agree that in the conception of true replica presupposed in the objection, there cannot be true replicas of historical objects. But all that follows from this is that when someone like Parfit talks of replication, if he is talking coherently and within the context of generally accepted conceptions of reality, he is not talking of true replication but only of replication of an object's current properties. And, of course, it is that conception of replication that was employed in my objection.

In fairness to Parfit, I think that many people, if they would reflect carefully on his many clarifying examples and arguments, would decide that physical continuity does not matter as much as they had thought it matters. The reason, I believe, is that for these people such reflection would tend to be transforming and liberalizing; or, perhaps, it would help them to realize that their values, all along, were more liberal than they thought they were. Whichever, I think that for many people the end product of the transformation or revelation that comes from studying Parfit's examples and arguments would be that their so-called egoistic survival values would be closer to Parfit's than to those the traditionalists recommend. I also think that such transformations or revelations would tend to be good since they would tend to be liberating. Hence, I'm deeply sympathetic with what I take to be Parfit's underlying point of view. I shall draw upon his reflections often in formulating my own alternative view. However, for present purposes, the crucial question is whether Parfit's arguments succeed in showing that a person rationally ought to have values like the ones he recommends. Partly because of the problems with his overall argumentative strategy that I have just been discussing, I think the answer to this question is, they do not.

Unger's Strategy

Unger (1991) has defended a "physically based" view of personal identity and of what matters in survival. He has argued not only that it is rationally permissible for physical continuity to matter primarily, but, more strongly, that it is rationally obligatory for it to matter primarily. Hence, he claimed that the pattern of values that Parfit argued is rationally required is actually irrational.

In Unger's view, first, the preservation of personal identity requires the persistence of one's core psychology (one's capacity for conscious experience, simple reasoning, and so on); and, second, the persistence of one's core psychology requires that it be physically realized continuously, not necessarily by a brain but by some physical realizer or other. Unger claims that all that basically ought to matter in survival (in his "prudential" sense of what matters, to be discussed in Chapter 3) is survival (identity) itself. He concedes that, derivatively, certain continuities that do not themselves suffice for survival ought to matter almost as much as survival itself. But according to him, "*Any* case that lacks strict survival will be worse than *every* case in which the person himself does survive" (1991, pp. 211–12; emphasis added). So, for instance, in his view, you would be irrational to think that undergoing a transformation that you correctly believe you would not strictly survive is nevertheless better (prudentially) than another option (*any* other option) you have in which you would strictly survive.

In my opinion, there are several problems with Unger's view. The problem with it that I want now to discuss concerns the argumentative strategy he uses to support his claim about the overriding rational/ prudential importance of survival. His strategy is to try to show, mainly by considering various spectra of examples in which cases of survival are compared with very similar cases in which survival is just barely lost, that the cases on these spectra that involve survival are always (prudentially) preferable to those that do not involve survival. In support of this view he uses a pain test by means of which he tries to show that we should always be willing to suffer more pain now to prevent *ourselves* from experiencing much greater pain later than we would be willing to suffer now to prevent someone who just barely missed being ourselves from suffering that same amount and kind of pain later.

On the face of it, there are problems with Unger's overall strategy for showing that *any* case that lacks strict survival is worse than *every* case that includes it. First, even if he were right that *we* – whoever "we" are – prudentially prefer outcomes in which we survive to extremely similar outcomes in which we barely miss surviving, that does not show that it would be irrational for someone else, who is not included in "our" group, either to be neutral between some such pairs of outcomes or even to prefer an outcome in which she did not survive; for, without her being irrational, strict survival may not be as valuable to her as Unger thinks it is to each of us. So far as I can tell, Unger has no argument that it would be irrational of someone else to have such values. But if there could be someone else who without irrationality has such values, then Unger needs an argument that it

25

would be irrational for one of us to abandon our current values and adopt this other person's values. He gives no such argument. Hence, the *most,* it seems, that he can show by his argumentative strategy is that we are irrational *if* we both retain our current values and prefer an outcome in which we survive to an outcome, no matter how otherwise similar, in which we do not survive. This conclusion, which ignores conversion, is much weaker and less interesting than the one for which he actually argues.

Second, assuming that Unger is right that, given our current values, we are committed (prudentially) to preferring outcomes in which we survive to *extremely similar* outcomes in which we barely miss surviving, that by itself cannot show that it would be irrational for us to prefer an outcome in which we do not survive to some *very different* outcome in which we do. For how we should judge the relative value of extremely similar outcomes has few interesting implications for how we should judge the value of very different outcomes.

If Unger's arguments based on spectra seem convincing, in my view it is because they are based almost exclusively on his comparing extremely similar pairs of outcomes. Assuming we value survival at all, which we do, then, of course, in considering extremely similar pairs of outcomes it will seem that to remain consistent with what we already value, we ought to prefer outcomes in which we survive to ones that are as similar as they can be in all other respects except that in them we do not survive. But the most Unger can show by such an argumentative strategy is that *all else being equal* we ought rationally to prefer survival to nonsurvival. Even were this true there may be cases in which all else is not equal and in which we are under no rational obligation to prefer survival to nonsurvival. That is, survival could be something we rationally value without its being something we value so much that its value necessarily overrides the value of everything else we rationally value. As we shall see in Chapters 3 and 4, there are examples which show that this is indeed the case and which thereby undermine Unger's arguments.

In sum, Parfit argues that *the mere fact that* some outcome preserves identity is not a good reason to prefer it to very similar outcomes that do not preserve identity. Whether or not his arguments for this conclusion are correct, a flaw in his strategy, as we have seen, is that he then infers from this conclusion that there are therefore *no good reasons* to prefer outcomes that preserve identity to very similar outcomes that do not. I have argued that even on the assumption that Parfit is right in his initial conclusion, he is mistaken in making this inference. That is, I have argued that there may well be reasons other than the one he considers – that is, the mere fact that an outcome preserves identity – to prefer outcomes that preserve identity. Unger, on the other hand, argues that the mere fact that some outcome preserves identity is a good reason to prefer it to very similar outcomes that do not preserve identity. He then illicitly infers from this conclusion that there are therefore always good reasons to prefer any outcome that preserves identity to any outcome that does not. I have argued that even on the assumption that he is right in his initial conclusion, he is mistaken in making this inference.

In my view, the arguments of Parfit and Unger on the question of what *ought* to matter in survival are as good as any that have been given. Yet these arguments do not work. Not only do they sometimes rest on mistaken assumptions (to be discussed later), but the overall strategies that both Parfit and Unger have employed are deeply flawed. And there is no way I know of to repair these flaws. The basic problem with both of their strategies is that within very broad limits it is much harder than Parfit and Unger realize to put rational constraints on what people can value.

The bottom line, then, seems to be that however attractive it may be to reach for some interesting, sweeping conclusion about what rationally ought to matter in survival, there is precious little evidence that any such conclusion is within our grasp. Of course, it is always open to someone to argue that there are better argumentative strategies to establish what ought to matter in survival than the ones I've considered, or to rebut my objections to Parfit and Unger's strategies, or to think of new and better ways of establishing some interesting, sweeping normative thesis about what rationally ought to matter in survival. Nothing I have said shows that one or another of these responses will not work. But for those, such as myself, who are deeply skeptical about whether any such response will work, it remains to ask whether there is a better way to address the question of what matters in survival.

RATIONALLY MOTIVATED CHANGES

For most of us, in certain kinds of cases, seeing mere linguistic conventions for what they are tends to erode their influence on our values and attitudes. For some of us, it tends to erode their influence deeply. And personal identity is one of these kinds of cases. These, I think, are just facts about our psychologies, that is, about the psychologies of the kinds of people who are likely to read this book. It is why Nozick was right to observe that the puzzle cases in the personal identity literature are koans for philosophers. Contemplating them tends to help people to understand personal identity more deeply, which in turn helps them to understand just how much our notions of personal identity depend on mere linguistic conventions, which, then, tends to diminish the value people place on personal identity.

Whether the erosion of merely conventional influences on one's values and attitudes will make one more rational and/or is a good thing are separate questions. As I've indicated, I think it is unlikely that anyone will ever show, in general, that eroding one's attachment to personal identity necessarily makes one more rational. What such an erosion of one's attachment may do, rather, is to make one's values and attitudes more sensitively responsive to underlying realities, that is, make them more in harmony with the way the world is. Assuming it does tend to do this, a question that arises is whether it is a good thing to have values and attitudes about personal identity that are more in harmony with the way the world is. And if it is a good thing, another question that arises is, Why?

Answering these questions is a delicate matter. In my opinion, in the case of personal identity, for most people and on the whole, the setting in motion of a rationally motivated transformation of people's most basic survival values that brings these values into closer harmony with the way the world is tends to be good for them. The reason it tends to be good is that it tends to be liberating (in a way that is itself a good thing), and this because certain common attachments to notions of self and identity imprison and harm people, not only by alienating them (see Parfit's "glass tunnel" metaphor, 1984, p. 281), but also by making them more fearful (e.g., of death). That bringing one's values into closer harmony with the way the world is does tend to have these consequences is difficult to explain and probably impossible to prove. I will not try to prove it. In Chapter 6 I try to explain it.

If I am right that it is a mistake to focus on the normative question of what ought to matter in survival, then it would seem that the most appropriate question is simply, What does matter? But there are problems with philosophers focusing mainly on this question. One problem is that as a question about what matters to the population at large, it is an empirical question that philosophers have no special competence to answer. Hence, it is best left to social psychologists. And even were philosophers competent to answer it, its answer may not be philosophically interesting. Most people have not thought much or deeply about their basic egoistic survival values. So, *philosophically* what does it matter what matters to them? Philosophically it would be more interesting, I think, to know what matters in survival to people who have thought deeply about their survival values. But, to me at least, even such an elitist social psychology would have limited philosophical interest.

What I primarily want to know about the broadly egoistic survival beliefs and values of others is not what matters to them but, rather, what (and how) various examples, discussions, arguments, criticisms, and so on have clarified their own understandings of themselves and their values. Information such as this could contribute directly to my acquiring a deeper understanding of my own beliefs and values. For instance, my own interest in the question of what matters in survival would not be diminished much if I came to believe that I would never know what other philosophers feel matters in survival to them. Although I am curious about what they feel matters in survival to them, what *primarily* interests me, rightly or wrongly, is understanding what matters in survival to me. I assume that some others have a similar egocentric focus.

Rationality plays a role in such an investigation in that I do not want my values to be based on misconceptions or mistakes, such as on my misguided acceptance of some bad theory. If the reasoning, distinctions, or self-knowledge that underlies my values, or what I take to be my values, is rationally defective, according to a criterion of rationality to which I subscribe, then I not only want to know that it is defective but I want the defect corrected. In addition, I do not want my values to arise from defective psychological processing, say, of a sort for which ordinary psychotherapy would be a desirable remedy. Otherwise, most – but not all – questions about the rationality of my so-called egoistic survival values are of decidedly less interest to me. A major reason for this is that attempts, however well-intentioned, to show something interesting about what we ought to value tend to slide all but inevitably into normative imperialism. Since, except rarely, philosophers cannot back up their claims that everyone else ought also to value what they themselves value, or what some group to which they belong values, why make such claims?

Some will question whether philosophers qua philosophers have any business setting in motion transformations of values that are not rationally obligatory. Why, they may ask, transform one's values in some way if we cannot show that they should be transformed in that way? There is no reason I can think of why one should transform one's values in any such way. But the suggestion is not that we transform our values but, rather, that we be open to allowing them to transform. Why, though, should we even want to do that? The answer, I think, is that if we allow our values to transform in response to a clearer understanding of who and what we are, of how our beliefs map onto reality, and of what the consequences are for ourselves and others of our having the values we have, then the values that emerge from such a transformation are likely to be better. In other words, when a change in one's values is rationally motivated, the new values that emerge are likely to be better at least for the person involved than the old values that have been discarded. Of course, this too is impossible to prove.

In sum, in my view, an important part of the philosophy of our most basic so-called egoistic survival values, that is, of what matters in survival, ought to be concerned with providing people with information about what might matter to them that could help them become clearer about their values. Greater clarity may – I think, often will – cause rationally motivated changes in what people value and/or in their attitudes. And for most people, I think, this would be a good thing. That is the project, and the rationale for the project, in this book.

2

Anticipation

Ever since John Locke, Western personal identity theorists have been preoccupied with looking at life backwards, through the lens of memory. Locke, for instance, used his prince and cobbler example to make the point that because someone might remember the experiences had by someone who inhabited a different body, people could switch bodies – a consideration thought by many to refute bodily continuity theories. As recently as the mid-1960s, bodily continuity theorists have tried to turn the tables by arguing that only genuine memories can sustain personal identity and only memories brought about by their normal physical causes can be genuine (Martin and Deutscher, 1966).

Beginning in the late 1960s, however, and increasingly since then, forward-looking perspectives have come to the fore, ushered in, as we have seen, by the consideration of fission examples. What makes fission examples so theoretically interesting is that they have seemed – and still do seem – to many to support the idea that people could lose their identities yet obtain what either should or does matter primarily to them in their so-called self-interested concern to survive. So, unlike the traditional (pre-1970s) debate, which, insofar as it influenced contemporary theory, focused almost exclusively on specifying the conditions under which identity is preserved, with memory as the primary focus of concern, more recently there have been the additional problems of trying to discover what should or does matter primarily in survival (with some still convinced it is identity), and then specifying the conditions under which that (whatever it is) obtains.

My interest is in this newer debate. I claim that there is an important source of self-concern – the anticipation of *having* experiences and of *performing* actions – that has either been overlooked or seriously underrated by major contributors to this debate and that, as a consequence, theories that were designed to challenge the idea that identity is what matters primarily in survival are weaker than they could be. To support this claim,

31

I shall critique the views of Derek Parfit (1984), Robert Nozick (1981), and John Perry (1976). Among the revolutionaries, these three have been the most influential theorists. In the end what I want to claim is that a person could anticipate having experiences that only someone else will have, anticipate having them in pretty much the same ways that most of us anticipate having only our own experiences, and be rational in doing so – an idea that, for brevity, I shall sometimes express simply as the idea that a person might rationally anticipate having experiences that only someone else will have. I think this idea is true. I also think it is applicable to many more sorts of situations than, I suspect, it will seem to many that it could be. And for pretty much the same reasons as in the case of anticipating having experiences, I think that a person could anticipate performing actions that only someone else will perform, anticipate performing them in pretty much the same ways that most of us anticipate performing only our own future actions, and be rational in doing so. I shall not argue for this latter claim.

THREE THEORIES

Parfit has argued for a closest-continuer account of personal identity, where psychological continuity and connectedness are the measures of closeness; and he has argued for a psychological continuity and connected-ness account of what matters in survival. Although he mentions explicitly only beliefs, memories, intentions, and character traits, presumably, in his view, every element of a person's psychology is relevant not only to whether a person persists, but also to whether what matters in that person's survival is preserved. To persist, in Parfit's view, a person, first, must be bound to someone at a later time by *enough* such psychological connec-tions and, second, may not be similarly bound to more than one person until after that time; that is, to persist, the relevant connections may not "branch." How *many* psychological connections must there be for one to have enough to persist? "Over *any* day *at least half* the number of direct connections that hold, over *every* day, in the lives of nearly every actual person" (1984, p. 222).

To preserve what matters in survival there must be the same sorts of psychological connections as in the case of personal identity. However, in the case of what matters in survival these connections may branch. Parfit does not say whether to preserve what matters in survival there is a similar requirement as in the case of identity on the number of connections that must obtain. There is little in the main body of his account, which has a

32

decidedly quantitative tone, to suggest otherwise. However, he does mention briefly that in the case of what matters in survival, qualitative differences among the connections also have to be taken into account (1984, pp. 209, 515n6). His view, then, is that what binds us are psychological connections, overlapping "like the strands in a rope" (p. 222). So far as identity is concerned, the more *numerous* the connections the stronger the rope. In the case of what matters in survival, however, it is not just the number of strands that counts, but also their length and thickness.

I agree that in the case of what matters in survival, not all psychological connections are equally important. Consider, for instance, the case of an American mother who as a consequence of undergoing some transformation forgot who was the fifth president of the United States or, even, most of what she knew about American history. Probably she would not feel that what matters in her survival had been compromised all that much. However, if instead she were to forget the names of her children, probably she would feel that what matters had been compromised a great deal (cf. Alzheimer's patients). Perhaps she would be mistaken in thinking that some memories are more important than others. Or perhaps her assessment could be explained on quantitative grounds, say, by counting the two sorts of lapsed psychological connections (assuming there were a way to do this) and then comparing the totals. However, it seems more plausible to suppose that her assessment is correct and that to account for what matters to her in her survival via psychological connectedness and/or continuity, the differing values to her of her psychological connections to herself at earlier times (or to earlier stages of herself) have to be taken into account. But, then, if we are going to go this far in trying to accommodate the actual pattern of peoples' differing values, why not also take into account the different values to them of their bodily connections to themselves at different times? Is it so clear that psychological connections are always more important?

Nozick also gives a closest-continuer account of identity and claims that (roughly equal) branching interferes with a person's persisting but not necessarily with a person's obtaining what matters primarily to him in survival. However, unlike Parfit, Nozick claims that in accounting for personal identity, the salient dimensions along which closeness should be measured should reflect the (prior) person's own values in survival and, hence, may be physical as well as psychological. This view of his implies, among other things, that some psychological connections might be more important than other psychological or bodily connections and that some bodily connections might be more important than other bodily or psychological connections. Yet Nozick says little about what sorts of connections actually do tend to matter. And like Parfit, he does not even mention the role that anticipating having someone's experiences may play in what matters.

Yet imagine that you were contemplating undergoing a transformation (say, teletransportation or fission). Suppose you did not believe that in so transforming you would preserve your identity but you wondered whether you would preserve what matters primarily to you in survival. It would be one thing for you to know *how many* of your beliefs, desires, intentions, memories, and so on would be preserved in the person (or people) who would emerge from the transformation. It would be quite another and, I think, an even more important thing to know whether your *most valued* psychological and bodily characteristics would be preserved in the person (or people) who would emerge from the transformation. And it would be still another thing to know whether you could look forward rationally to *having* the experiences (and *performing the actions*) of the person (or people) who would emerge from the transformation. To me this latter consideration would be at least as important as each of the other two.

What I am suggesting is that if you are like me in this respect, then if you could *not* rationally anticipate having the experiences that at least one of your transformational descendants would have, then, from the perspective of your self-interested concern to survive, something crucial would be missing, regardless of how else you and your descendants might be connected; and if you could rationally anticipate having the experiences that at least one of your descendants would have, something of extraordinary and perhaps overriding importance would obtain, regardless of whatever other connections might be missing. If this is not obvious, it may become so by considering Perry's account. For while he sometimes recognizes the importance of anticipating having someone else's experiences, his account is vulnerable to criticism precisely because he fails to integrate this insight into his view.

Perry's main objective is to explain and assess the rationality of the "special reasons" each of us has to care, and to care in the ways we do, about ourselves in the future: "You learn that someone will be run over by a truck tomorrow; you are saddened, feel pity, and think reflectively about the frailty of life; one bit of information is added, that the someone is you, and a whole new set of emotions rise in your breast" (1976, p. 67). In Perry's view, if we have good reasons to care especially about ourselves in the future, and to care in the ways we do, it is because it is much more likely that we will promote our own "projects" than that others will promote our projects. For example, if I know that by pushing a button I will prevent myself from being in great pain tomorrow, then I almost surely have more reason to push it than if I know simply that by pushing it I will prevent someone from being in great pain tomorrow: "If I am not in pain tomorrow, I will contribute to the 'success' of many of my projects: I will work on this article, help feed my children, and so forth. If I am in great pain, I will not do some of these things" (p. 74). In Perry's view, the special concern each of us has for ourselves in the future is derivative, rather than fundamental, because insofar as this concern is rational, it can be explained in terms of our desires that projects be completed – projects that could, in principle, be completed by others.

In elaborating his account Perry distinguishes between what he calls "private projects" and the "ego project." A private project is one I may have "to which I will (or may) make a contribution that no one else could make"; for instance, I may want not only that an article I am writing be completed but that it be completed by *me*. The ego project is a private project I may have to which "I will be in a position to make my special contribution no matter what I am like tomorrow"; for instance, I may want simply to be "alive, whatever I may be like, whatever I may remember, whatever desires I may then have" (1976, pp. 78–9).

Perry says that in normal circumstances when we want to be the ones to complete our private projects it is because, if we don't complete them but someone else does, "that could only be because of a variety of catastrophes, which will leave other projects uncompleted and this one, perhaps, ill completed" (1976, p. 79). But in that case we are, he thinks, only derivatively justified in having private projects. In the example, say, of my private project that I finish the article on which I have been working, fundamentally I have only the nonprivate project that the article be completed, which I upgrade to a private project because if I do not work on completing the article, other of my (ultimately nonprivate) projects will also fail. What Perry thinks shows that in normal circumstances my justification in having private projects is derivative is that in certain exotic circumstances no such justification is available. For instance, if in otherwise normal circumstances I were to cease and be replaced by an exact replica, then not only my article but everything I will do tomorrow and for the rest of my life could be done as well, as quickly, and in the same way by someone else.

Perry concedes that most of us if we were suddenly confronted with such exotic circumstances still may want that we – and not some "benign imposter" – complete the article. However, in such exotic circumstances

35

there is no justification, he claims, for our wanting this. We would want it, he says, because we have two habits, formed in normal circumstances, that we import inappropriately into the exotic circumstances. One is that we tend to believe that surviving is the only way to ensure the completion of our projects. The other is that we tend to identify only with ourselves in the future; that is, we tend to imagine from the inside what the future experiences only of ourselves will be like. Perry speculates that the habit of identifying only with ourselves, which in ordinary circumstances is so useful for achieving our purposes, is ingrained in us by the demands of evolution (1976, p. 80).

In commenting on the ego project, Perry imagines what it would be like if tomorrow a person was to be struck by amnesia "incurable in fact, though not in principle; that my character and personality will suddenly change, so I will hate what I now love, and work against what I now hope for" (1976, p. 84). Perry asks what special reasons he would have to care about such a person due to that person's being himself. He answers: none whatsoever. Why then under such circumstances would most of us still care? He answers: habit. "We take identity always to be a good reason for care and concern because usually it is" (p. 84).

In spite of its many virtues Perry's account of our reasons for special concern is seriously incomplete. To return to his initial example, generally you will have more reason to prevent your own pain tomorrow than you will simply to prevent someone's pain, not, as Perry would have it, primarily because preventing your own pain will be more likely to promote your projects – at least not the sort of projects Perry usually mentions. Rather, you will have more reason to prevent your own pain tomorrow because, as you believe, your own pain will hurt you and someone else's pain either won't hurt you or won't hurt you as badly (since, as you believe, you will experience having your own pain directly but experience having another's pain only indirectly, if at all). Imagine, for instance, that you were told convincingly that for thirty minutes tomorrow you would suffer excruciating pain. Probably you would dread the prospect. How much would it help if you were then told that the pain would not come while you were actively promoting your projects but during an idle half-hour when you weren't doing much that matters to you anyway? Probably, upon being given this extra item of information, you would not feel that much better. Would it help, then, to be told that although the pain would be genuinely excruciating, much worse than anything you have ever experienced, neither the anxiety that it is coming nor its effect on you after it comes would make much difference to how much you were able to get done either during the rest of the day or subsequently? Again, if you are like me, while this new information might help a little, the key words would be, "genuinely excruciating, much worse than anything you have ever experienced." So long as I thought excruciating pain was on the way, the new information would not provide much relief. Nor, it seems, should it.

Now consider a variation on this example. Suppose that between noon and 1 P.M. tomorrow you and another person have planned to work jointly on a project to which both of you are likely to contribute equally. You learn that throughout that hour one of you will experience continuously an excruciating pain of a certain sort. You've had that sort of pain before and, so, know what it feels like. Since that pain is about all the person who has it will experience while he is having it, he will make no contribution to the joint project. However, after the hour is over neither of you will remember that the pain occurred, but instead both of you will, incorrectly, seemingly remember that the reason you got only half as much done on the project as you had thought you would get done is that an unknown prankster kept setting off the fire alarm in your building. Otherwise neither of you – and no one else – will be affected by the pain's having been experienced.

Since the pain is a familiar one to you and is about all the person who has it will experience, you can identify (suppose), in Perry's sense of "identify," with the person who experiences the pain just as much if that person were your partner as if that person were yourself; that is, either way you can imagine as well from the inside what that person's experience will be like. Under these circumstances, would you have any special egoistic reasons for wishing that it be the other person who experiences the pain and not you? Surely you would: namely, that, as you believe, your own pain will hurt you and someone else's pain either won't hurt you or won't hurt you in the same way or as badly. There are no resources in Perry's account for explaining or for justifying your having these special reasons. Perhaps it would not be rational for you to feel these ways. But if it would not be, it has to be shown that it would not be and why; and the virtually universal presence among people of such reasons for special concern would have to be explained.

In sum, contrary to Perry's account, the explanation for our preferring that we and not some benign imposter complete our projects is not simply the sorts of habitual beliefs that Perry mentions, but includes as well, and crucially, our belief that if a benign imposter were to complete our projects, then we would not have the experience of completing them. To convince yourself of this just remember (or imagine) some time when you were lusting passionately after someone you deeply loved. Now ask yourself, sticking to Perry's terminology (which, in the case of this example, is unfortunate), whether you wanted just that the "project" of *someone's* making love to this person be "completed"; or, whether you wanted *also* that *you* be the one to "complete" that "project"; or whether you wanted in addition, and crucially, that you *have the experience* of "completing" it. Surely the latter. But if so, then it would seem that by overemphasizing the importance of "completing projects," Perry has failed to get all the way to the experiential roots of self-concern.

Even in those aspects of Perry's account where he is most experiential, he does not attend sufficiently to the difference between imagining someone's experiences "from the inside" and anticipating having those experiences. For instance, he says that "a person *identifies* with the participant in a past, future, or imaginary event when he imagines perceiving the event from the perspective of the participant," say, by imagining seeing and hearing what the participant sees and hears as the event in question occurs (1976, p. 75). But as I argue in Chapter 5, this way of understanding identification lumps together what for theories of what matters in survival are crucially different cases. One is that of identifying with another person, say, by being empathic in a certain way but without anticipating *having* that person's experiences, and the other is identifying with someone by anticipating having his experiences.

Ironically, the idea of anticipating having someone's experiences may get its clearest expression from Perry in his introductory textbook account, where in the last paragraph Cohen asks the dying Gretchen Weirob to imagine an operation that would preserve her brain but not, in Gretchen's view, her identity, but which she decides to undergo anyway. Cohen asks Gretchen to imagine that as the time for the imagined operation approaches,

> you go ahead and anticipate the experiences of the survivor. Where exactly is the mistake? Do you really have any less reason to care for the survivor than for yourself? Can mere identity of body, the lack of which alone keeps you from being her, mean that much? Perhaps we were wrong, after all in focusing on identity as the necessary condition of anticipation. (Perry, 1978, p. 49)

This, I think, is close to the key issue. Yet even here, as we saw also in his account of identification, Perry does not distinguish sharply between anticipating (or imagining) an experience and anticipating having that experience and, hence, fails to weight properly the important appropriative aspect of the latter. In any case, his *Dialogue* ends at that point. Perry neither endorses the idea that someone might rationally anticipate having someone else's experiences nor, so far as I know, discusses it further.

The problem with Perry's account of our "special reasons" for being concerned about ourselves in the future is not just that he shortchanges the anticipation of *having* experiences. He also fails to discuss other egoistic motives that may be relevant. Among these are our desires to be responsible and to receive appropriate credit for completing our "projects." Consider, for instance, his example of someone's finishing an article. A person may want that he be the one to finish it so that he personally is responsible for its being finished and/or so that he gets credit appropriately for its being finished. People may feel, perhaps rightly, that if the article were to be completed by a benign imposter, instead of by themselves, they would be deprived of both these benefits. Since I think the experience issue is by far a more important concern than that of responsibility or credit, I shall emphasize experience in what follows. However, in Objection 6, I return to the issue of responsibility.

EIGHT OBJECTIONS

Ordinarily there would be a huge difference between how it would feel to you to anticipate your having an experience and how it would feel to you to anticipate, or look forward to, someone else's having a very similar experience, say, between how it would feel to you to anticipate your enjoying a delicious dinner and how it would feel to you to anticipate my enjoying that same dinner. There would be this huge difference even if you thought that my experience would be qualitatively identical to yours. The difference might be diminished somewhat if the person whose experiences you anticipated were someone, such as your spouse or one of your children, with whom you were strongly empathically connected. Even so, under normal circumstances it would be odd if both sorts of anticipations were to feel the same. It is natural to assume that a person would have to be demented or irrational, or in the distorting grip of some bizarre philosophical theory, to think that he might rationally anticipate *having* experiences that only someone else will have. Yet, however natural this assumption, it is not easy, as the following survey will show, to come up with even one good, non-question-begging objection to the idea that a person could rationally anticipate having experiences that only someone else will have.

Objection 1. It is a conceptual truth that people can rationally anticipate having only their own future experiences.

Reply. This has never been shown. To show it, one would have to appeal to ordinary linguistic usage, and it is unclear how ordinary usage either applies or should be extended to apply to many of the puzzle cases envisaged in the personal identity literature. However, even if it were a conceptual truth that people can rationally anticipate having only their own future experiences, it would be a conceptual truth only relative to certain concepts or models (say, of rationality). It would always be open to us to modify or discard our concepts or models.

Not too long ago many philosophers thought it was a conceptual truth that pain hurts. Suppose, for the sake of argument, that they were right. Even so, recent research encourages us to separate the question of whether someone is in pain from that of whether their being in pain hurts them. In certain unusual but actual circumstances, such as under the power of hypnotic suggestion, people can accurately assess the varying intensity of pain that is their own even though it is not distressful to them (Hilgard, 1977). It is a short and arguably a relatively easy step from this finding to the conclusion that in certain circumstances pain may not hurt.

The general moral is that to accommodate theoretical advances, conceptual constraints may be revised. There is no reason to think that whatever conceptual constraints govern the rational anticipation of having experiences are immune to revision. In any case, this objection, based as it is merely on linguistic considerations, is easily avoided by defining a notion of *quasi-anticipation,* like the notion of anticipation in every respect except that there is no conceptual requirement that people quasi-anticipate only their own experiences. Since this move is available and meets the objection, I shall continue to talk in terms of people anticipating having the experiences others will have. Anyone who is bothered by ordinary language objections to such talk may substitute in the claims that follow a suitably defined notion of quasi-anticipation.

Objection 2. Necessarily when people anticipate having their own future experiences, they anticipate *their* having them. It is self-contradictory to say that people might anticipate their having an experience that only others will have. For people to have the experiences of others they would have to be those others, which ex hypothesi they are not.

40

Reply. This objection rests on a misconception. The proposal is not that people might rationally anticipate *their* having experiences that will be had only by others but, rather, that they might rationally anticipate others' having experiences yet anticipate the experiences in pretty much the same ways that most of us anticipate having our own experiences. Parfit, for instance, asked us to imagine an example in which Jane seems to remember Paul's experience, in Venice, of looking across water and seeing a lightening bolt fork and strike both the bell tower of San Georgio and the red funnel of a passing tugboat (Parfit, 1984, p. 220). Parfit claimed that in seeming to remember this experience, Jane might have known she was seeming to remember an experience that Paul had had and that if she had known this, then she would have known, from the inside, part of what it was like to be Paul on that day in Venice. In other words, Jane would have known that she was seeming to remember Paul's experience from the same sort of subjective point of view from which Paul actually had the experience and from which ordinarily Jane actually remembers only her own experiences. If Jane had known this, she would have known she was seeming to remember having Paul's experience. But if, as it does, it makes sense to suppose that someone seems to *remember having* an experience that only someone else had, then why shouldn't it also make sense that one might *anticipate having* an experience that only someone else will have?

Some may doubt whether people could have any such anticipatory concern for others, on the grounds that if the notion of quasi-anticipation were the mirror image of quasi-memory, it would be too wide a notion. But imagine a fission case in which the donor's brain is divided into functionally equivalent halves, each of which is capable of sustaining her full psychology, and then each half is implanted into a replica body qualitatively identical to the donor's body. Suppose that immediately after the fission one of the replicas is put into an unconscious coma and kept in a hospital while the other leads a normal life. Suppose also that the donor knows before the fission occurs that this is what will happen (in the next chapter, I develop a fuller version of this example).

Before the fission occurs, such a donor would have two bases for anticipating having her conscious replica's experiences: She would know that the very same casual mechanisms that will underlie her replica's experiences now underlie her own experiences; and she could imagine from the inside what her conscious replica's experiences would be like as well as, and in all the same ways as, normally she can imagine from the inside her own future experiences. The satisfaction of these two conditions would justify the donor's anticipating having her conscious replica's experiences since, linguistic conventions aside, these two conditions are the same ones that now justify the actual anticipations people have of having their own future experiences.

If people cannot be rationally entitled to anticipate having experiences that will be had only by others, then the revolutionary program that identity should not be what matters primarily in survival is in deep trouble. For if identity is not to matter, then it is going to have to be permissible for us to be connected affectively to others as closely as, and in the same ways as, normally we are connected affectively only to ourselves. If we cannot anticipate having the experiences of others, then few of us would be able to be connected affectively nearly as closely to these others as we are to ourselves. And, hence, we would have lost something that is important. For instance, assume that in a teletransportation process your teletransported replica will be another person, that you know he will soon experience great pain, and that you are worried about his having to experience this pain. Is your worry the same sort of worry that normally you would have only for yourself in the future, say, of dreading his having to experience pain? Or is your worry of the sort that normally you would have only for others – do you merely pity him for having to experience the pain? If you merely pity him for having to experience the pain, then unless it can be shown that you shouldn't even dread your own forthcoming pain, you won't be as closely connected to him as you would have been to yourself in the future. And if you cannot be as closely connected affectively to someone else in the future as you can be to yourself, why should anyone agree that identity is not (i.e., should not be) what matters primarily in survival? Don't affective connections matter?

Objection 3. The idea that someone might rationally anticipate having someone else's experience is self-refuting. If someone were rationally to anticipate having an experience that someone in the future will have and our criteria of rationality are fixed, we would thereby be provided with sufficient reason to adopt criteria of personal identity that ensure that the anticipator and the person whose experiences she anticipates having are the same person.

Reply. Not necessarily. There could be reasons for retaining criteria of personal identity that do not preclude the possibility that someone might rationally anticipate having an experience that only someone else will have. For instance, if it were to turn out that there were no basis for putting any limitations on whose future experiences a person might rationally anticipate having (i.e., whose experiences, as judged by currently accepted criteria of personal identity), then to modify our criteria of personal identity so as to block the possibility that one might rationally anticipate having experiences that only someone else will have, we would have to accept the view that there is just one person. Faced with this consequence we might prefer to retain stricter criteria of personal identity and concede that the anomalous sort of rational anticipation might be realized.

Objection 4. Even if we were to allow that people might rationally anticipate having experiences that only others will have, we could not allow that they could anticipate having those experiences in pretty much the same ways that ordinarily people anticipate having only their own future experiences. The tie between the anticipation of having an experience and identity is so central to ordinary ways of anticipating having an experience that any departure from this constraint would guarantee that the anomalous anticipation would be radically different.

Reply. Perhaps not. Ordinary anticipation is a complex process, the physical details of which are unknown. Currently there is no reason to think that an adequate theory of anticipation, were we to have one, would sustain this objection. For all we know, there may not be any elements of actual anticipation that are essentially linked to anticipators identifying the future experiencers as themselves.

Objection 5. Anticipation looks toward the future. It is the analog of memory, which looks toward the past. To avoid nonsense we have to assume that the person who remembers having an experience and the person who originally had the experience are the same person. For similar reasons we have to assume that the person anticipating having an experience and the person whose experience he anticipates having are the same person.

Reply. It is true that we need a constraint on memory to preserve the distinction between genuine and mere seeming (but nevertheless correct) memory. However, for a variety of reasons, we cannot preserve this distinction properly by insisting that the rememberer and the person who had the experience remembered are the same; rather, we can preserve it only by insisting that there be some appropriate causal, or perhaps subjunctive, link between the rememberer and the person who had the experience remembered. In any case, when it comes to anticipation, the only distinction we want to preserve that might be analogous to that between genuine and mere seeming memory is that between rational and irrational anticipation. And there are many possible ways of preserving this latter distinction. For instance, we can preserve the distinction between rational and irrational anticipation simply by saying that anticipations are irrational if anticipators should have known they had insufficient evidence that the anticipated experiences would occur.

Even if it were true that to avoid some sort of nonsense we need additional constraints on whose experiences one might rationally anticipate having, we might be able to get by with constraints that do not require that anticipators are the same people as those whose experiences they anticipate having. For instance, we might require only that there is a continuer relationship of some sort between anticipators and the people whose experiences they anticipate having – a relationship that is either not sufficiently close or not of the right sort to sustain identity. To see how this might work consider a variation on the objection under consideration.

Objection 6.   Anticipating having experiences that only someone else will have would lead inevitably to inappropriate emotions and feelings of responsibility. Consider, first, a retrospective example, involving quasi-memories. Imagine, say, someone who has quasi-memories of doing many things that Napoleon actually did. Suppose that from a phenomenological point of view his experience is what Napoleon's would have been had Napoleon been put in suspended animation, awakened in the present, and given a conscience. As a result, the person who has such quasi-memories is tortured by guilt, desires to be punished, and is constantly suicidal. Even so, he has no false beliefs; for instance, he does not believe that his body is continuous with Napoleon's, that they both share the same immaterial soul, or that his "memories" were formed in the usual way. Rather, he believes correctly that the relevant aspects of his phenomenology are the result of quasi-memories produced by his imagination operating unconsciously in conjunction with what he has read and heard about Napoleon.

Suppose that these beliefs that the subject has about the source of his present quasi-memories do not undermine their phenomenology. And because of the subject's philosophical views (suppose he was corrupted by having read an earlier draft of the present book), his beliefs about the formation of his quasi-memories do not even undermine his belief at the theoretical level that he is justified in feeling guilt and remorse. Even so, the subject's guilt and remorse are *unjustified*. Compassionate people who knew all the facts would want that his guilt and remorse be alleviated through appropriate therapeutic means. They would distinguish between this subject and Napoleon, even though the phenomenologies of the two were exactly parallel. And they would feel differently about the appropriateness in the two cases of the phenomenology and of the accompanying disposition to sacrifice.

But if this example is convincing, an analogous future-oriented example involving anticipation should for the same reasons also be convincing. Suppose, for instance, that a person anticipated with horror having the sadistic pleasure that another person, who would be born after the subject died, would have as a consequence of committing some terrible crime. Suppose also that the earlier person by so anticipating caused herself tremendous anxiety as well as a kind of prospective guilt and remorse. Under conditions parallel to those that obtained in the preceding example, wouldn't we feel that the subject's anxiety, guilt, and remorse were inappropriate and, if possible, should be relieved by therapy?

Reply. In the case of the person who has quasi-memories of doing many things that Napoleon actually did and who as a consequence feels guilt and remorse, most of us would feel that the guilt and remorse are unjustified. But what if the quasi-rememberer's connections with Napoleon were closer than in the case of the person in that example, though not close enough for him actually to be Napoleon. For instance, suppose that late in life Napoleon fissioned into two descendants. Suppose also, for the sake of argument, that we are three-dimensionalists about people and hence believe that Napoleon's fission caused him to cease and be replaced by descendants who are different people. Finally, suppose that one of Napoleon's fission descendants subsequently acquired a conscience and as a consequence felt guilt and remorse for what Napoleon had done. What attitude would we take toward this fission descendant's feelings of guilt and remorse? I think it would be possible to elaborate this example (perhaps in a way parallel to the "fission rejuvenation" example to be discussed in the next chapter) so that many of us would feel, and be justified in feeling, that such a fission descendant's guilt and remorse were just as appropriate as

Napoleon's would have been if instead of fissioning he had simply acquired a conscience and as a consequence felt guilty and remorseful himself. In sum, although in the original version of the example the person's connection to Napoleon was not close enough to justify his feelings of guilt and remorse, it is unwarranted simply to assume that for him to have been close enough so that those feelings were justified, he would have to have been Napoleon.

Similarly with the prospective example described in the objection. The question is whether there are any circumstances, real or imagined, in which we would think that it would be appropriate for a person to anticipate, with horror, having the sadistic pleasure that another person (who would be born after the subject ceased) would have as a consequence of committing some terrible crime. Perhaps there are. Suppose the subject's cessation came about not through ordinary death but as a consequence of his having fused with another person. Suppose further that the sadistic pleasure the subject anticipated having was going to be had by the subject's fusion descendant (perhaps as a consequence of that descendant's retaining certain undesirable aspects of the subject's psychology, rather than those of the psychology of the other person who fused or as a consequence of the fusion itself). In such a case, might not the subject's horror be appropriate?

Two caveats are in order. First, it would be a delicate matter to figure out what the conditions are under which people in such imaginary circumstances would and would not appropriately feel guilt, remorse, horror, responsibility, and so on. I do not pretend to have done this. My point, rather, is that it would be unwarranted to assume without much more argument than is given in the objection that the line between self and other would be a fundamental part of any account that does appropriately specify those conditions. Second, it may seem that to reply adequately to the sort of objection raised, I would have to assume, as I did assume in my reply, a three-dimensionalist view of persons. I do not think I would. In Chapter 4, I explain how the same sorts of doubts that theorists have raised about the importance of identity by using fission (or fusion) examples and assuming a three-dimensionalist view of persons can be raised as well without fission (or fusion) examples and without assuming a three-dimensionalist view of persons. My explanation of this requires a careful setup and it would be a distraction to try to deal here with the issues it raises.

Objection 7. Anticipating having experiences that only someone else will have would lead inevitably to dysfunctional and, therefore, irrational behavior. For instance, anticipating, when you are hungry, having someone else's experience of enjoying a full meal would rob you of your motivation to eat. It might even lead you to starve. More generally, if people frequently were to anticipate having experiences that only others will have, it would seriously undermine their motivation to enhance the quality of their own future experiences and, hence, undermine their motivation to promote their own welfare, perhaps even their own survival.

Reply. Whether anticipating having experiences that only someone else will have would be dysfunctional depends, among other things, on what one means by *dysfunctional.* It also depends on what sort of restrictions, if any, are put on whoever's experiences one might rationally anticipate having and on the conditions that must obtain for one rationally to anticipate having them. It would be hard to argue plausibly, and without begging the question, that a conservatively restricted version of the idea that someone might rationally anticipate having experiences that only someone else will have necessarily would lead to dysfunctional behavior. Consider, for instance, Parfit's example of a person contemplating teletransporting to Mars (Parfit, 1984, pp. 199–200). Whether the person's choosing to teletransport would be dysfunctional depends, among other things, on whether, in teletransporting, the person would preserve what matters primarily to him in his self-interested concern to survive. One of the chief things on which that would depend, I have claimed, is whether the person could rationally anticipate having the experiences that his teletransported replica would subsequently have. It would be question-begging simply to assume that he could not rationally anticipate having those experiences.

Objection 8. Once you remove the requirement that people can rationally anticipate having only their own future experiences, there is no defensible way to reinstate a restriction on whose future experiences people could rationally anticipate having. Rejecting the commonsense restriction on rational anticipation puts one on a slippery slope that leads inexorably to the result that one could rationally anticipate having anyone's, or even everyone's, subsequent experiences. And, on *any* reasonable criterion of dysfunctionality, the disposition to anticipate having everyone's subsequent experiences surely would be dysfunctional, and, hence, on *any* reasonable criterion of rationality, it would also be irrational.

Reply. I agree that the real issue is whether there are empirical, particularly consequentialist, grounds for putting restrictions on whose experiences people can rationally anticipate having and/or on the conditions under which people can rationally anticipate having them. Maybe departing from common sense would put one on a slippery slope that leads inexorably to unacceptable results. Maybe not. So far as I know, no one has shown that it would. We have already seen that on this issue one can depart from common sense quite a bit without necessarily allowing patterns of behavior that are dysfunctional on all plausible criteria of dysfunctionality. How far one can depart and in what ways are separate questions. In my view, it is surprisingly difficult to justify the claim that one could not depart far.

Consider, first, a person on his deathbed, who anticipates having experiences that someone else, who does not yet exist, will have after he – the deathbed anticipator – dies. Suppose, say, that the deathbed anticipator anticipates being reborn as his niece's first child (such an anticipation would not be unusual in some Eskimo cultures). Surely a dying person's anticipating having the experiences that his niece's first child will have need not (though it may) have bad consequences. In general, when anticipators cease to exist prior to the time when the people whose experiences they anticipate having begin to exist and the anticipations do not themselves play a role in the anticipators' ceasing to exist, the anticipations *may* well be harmless.

Suppose, next, that the lives of the anticipators and the lives of the people whose experiences they anticipate having do not overlap but that the anticipations play a role in the anticipators' ceasing to exist. Suppose, say, that had the anticipators not believed it was rational to anticipate having other peoples' experiences, they would not have initiated some process – such as teletransportation – that resulted in their cessations. Even so, this does not imply that their anticipations were irrational. Under the circumstances we cannot, without begging the question, assume that either their cessations or anything else are harms to the anticipators that *must* have resulted from their anticipations. If people do not persist through fission, similar remarks could be made about the donors' (in certain fission examples) anticipating having experiences that will be had by their fission descendants.

Problems caused by people anticipating having experiences that only others will have are more likely to arise when the two lives overlap. But, even then, problems are not inevitable, not even in the case of some of the sorts of examples that it might seem would be most problematic. For instance, what would be the likely consequences for someone of anticipating having another's experience of being pleasantly satisfied one evening after the other ate dinner? Would the anticipator lose interest in eating her own dinner? If the anticipator regularly anticipated having the other's experiences of being satisfied after eating and the other ate regularly, would the anticipator starve?

The answers to such questions depend on how anticipating having another's experiences would affect an anticipator's motivation to eat. And no one knows. Anticipators might act differently in response to their anticipating having the experiences of others who are not among their continuers than they would in response to their anticipating having the experiences of their own continuers. If so, then even if someone were to anticipate having another's experience of being pleasantly satisfied after the other ate dinner (assuming, now, that this other is not among the anticipator's continuers), that anticipation might not cause the anticipator to refrain from eating, in which case no harm would have to come to the anticipator from her anticipating having the other's experience.

If it seems far-fetched that no harm would have to come to such anticipators, consider the experiences that normal people actually have that are most like anticipating having experiences that others will have, namely, feelings of being empathic (or sympathetic) about something that others will experience. Even very empathic people may not, by their being empathic, harm either themselves or others. On the contrary, the world might be a better place if almost all of us were quite a bit more empathic than we are. For instance, when relatively affluent people hear that there is a famine somewhere, it might actually be better, on balance, if they anticipated having the suffering that the famine sufferers will have as vividly as they would anticipate having their own future suffering were they, themselves, to be facing famine. They might, then, try harder to help.

Empathy can be carried to unhealthy extremes. People can take the weight of the world on their shoulders in a way that undermines their motivation to look after their own welfare. But empathy, even extreme empathy, does not necessarily undermine one's motivation to look after oneself (think, for instance, of Mother Theresa). The reason, apparently, is that the motivations of psychologically healthy people are not generally affected in all of the same ways by feelings even of extreme empathy as they are by their anticipations of having their own future experiences. As with empathy, so also, perhaps, with anticipating having another's experiences.

It may seem, though, that there is another sort of harm that inevitably would result if the lives of the anticipator and of the other overlapped, namely, that the anticipator's expectation of having the other's experiences would inevitably be frustrated. It would distort a person's psychology to ignore past failures and continue to anticipate having someone else's experiences in the teeth of continual frustration. This is a genuine worry not easily answered. However, it rests on debatable assumptions about what the life of a person would be like who regularly anticipated having experiences that only others would have. Since the discussion of these assumptions would take us too far afield and it is not necessary to go into them to make the more restricted point that at least under certain conditions a person might without bad consequences anticipate having experiences that only others will have, I shall not pursue this question.

WHY ANTICIPATING HAVING IS SO IMPORTANT

When it comes to looking forward to what may happen, anticipating having our own future experiences is one of the most significant ways we can be connected to ourselves in the future. For similar reasons, anticipating having others' experiences would be one of the most significant ways we could be connected to others in the future. But why should anticipating *having* others' experiences be so much more meaningful than merely expecting *that* others will have certain experiences?

There are, I think, two main reasons. First, when we anticipate having others' experiences, we anticipate what they will experience from the same subjective points of view from which they will experience it, at least if our anticipations are borne out and the others do have the anticipated experiences. This is how we normally anticipate only our own future experiences, and it is a much more intimate – since "internal" – way of being connected now to people in the future than merely expecting that they will have some sort of experience, which is how we normally anticipate the experiences of others.

Second, the anticipation of having others' experiences requires that the anticipators identify with the others, not in the sense that the anticipators regard the others as the same people as themselves, but in some sense close to that. It requires that the anticipators identify in the sense that many of their dispositions that normally take only themselves as their object now take the others as their object. So, for instance, the anticipators may dread the suffering they expect the others to suffer or long for the pleasure they expect the others to experience in pretty much the same ways that the anticipators would dread their own future suffering or long for their own future pleasure. In other words, in anticipating having others' experiences the anticipators may react affectively toward those people and their (imagined) experiences as if those people were themselves and those peoples' experiences were their own, even though they know those people are others.

By pale analogy, die-hard sports fans watching the big game on TV may shout, "We've got to score," even though they know that, if scoring gets done, it will be the team, not them, that does it. Still, in adopting the team as "their own" the fans become disposed in certain respects to regard the team as a surrogate for themselves. As a consequence, so far as many of the fans' affective dispositions are concerned, it is to some extent as if they and the team were one. Thus, fans may feel proud of the team's successes as if these were their own successes or feel outraged by the team's being "unfairly" penalized as if they, themselves, were the immediate victims, and so on. Of course, normally fans would not anticipate having the team's experiences (whatever, exactly, that might mean) and so would not in that respect regard the team as a surrogate for themselves. Nevertheless, such identification, whether with a person, a team, an institution, or whatever, can be the polar opposite of the alienating negative feeling of not being included within the circle of something one values, that is, of "not belonging." That is one of the main reasons why this sort of identification is such an important locus of value in our lives.

In sum, rationally anticipating having others' experiences, while it does not imply that the anticipators and the people who are expected to have the experiences are the same people or even that the anticipators believe they are the same people, usually ensures that the connection between the anticipators and the people who are expected to have the experiences is close enough to secure many of the benefits (and also the drawbacks) of identity: an intimate ("internal") connection to the people whose experiences are anticipated, identification with those people, and so on. That is why any account of what matters in survival had better give due weight to the anticipation of having experiences. The price of not doing so is that the relations specified in the theory are doomed to seem less robust (in a way that diminishes their value) than is identity itself. In other words, the only way that an account of what matters in survival can specify relations, which even though they do not include identity, seem almost as important as identity, is by including among these relations the anticipation of having experiences; otherwise, even if the relations specified are accepted as the next best thing to being there, their obtaining is not likely either to be or to seem to be nearly as good as being there. However, when the anticipation of having experiences is included among these relations, then the relations stand a much better chance — in some cases, as we shall see, an excellent chance — of not only being but also seeming to be almost as good as being there.

3

Rejuvenation

I want now to introduce a kind of fission example that I claim is invulnerable to recent neoconservative attempts to show that identity really is what matters in survival. I shall use the example to support two ideas: first, that for many people identity is not what matters primarily; and, second, that for those same people there is no reason to think that identity should be what matters primarily. In arguing for these ideas I shall assume that the question of what matters in survival is best approached from a thoroughly naturalistic perspective, hence, that personal identity is not best explained by appeal to spiritual substances, to immaterial souls, to any sort of supposedly essentially indivisible entity, and so on. All of the neoconservatives whose views I am going to consider would grant such assumptions.

THE EXAMPLE: FISSION REJUVENATION

John is twenty years old. Physically and psychologically he is in very good shape. He is handsome, healthy, and vital. He knows that even without undergoing fission rejuvenation his prospects are good for a long and happy life. He also knows that he will never be in better physical condition, never better positioned, to undergo the procedure. He worries that already he may have waited too long.

In the morning John will go to the hospital, where he will be put under a general anesthetic and then have his brain divided into functionally equivalent halves, each capable of sustaining his full psychology. Each half of his brain will then be put into a body of its own that is qualitatively identical to his prefission body, which will then be destroyed. Hours later, one of his fission descendants, A, will wake up in the recovery room and begin a painless, two-week-long recovery after which he will leave the hospital in excellent health, looking and feeling like John looked and felt just prior to his undergoing the procedure. Except for such differences as are occasioned by A's knowing that the procedure took place and that

John's other fission descendant, B, also exists, A's subsequent physical and psychological development (and ultimate decay) will be like John's would have been had John not undergone the procedure.

B will have a different fate. Before he awakens from the anesthetic he will be administered a drug that will put him into a deep, dreamless coma. The drug will preserve B's body in its initial state until he is awakened. As it happens that will not be for another fifty-five years. Throughout these years B will be kept safely in the hospital.

During the operation a small device hooked up to a tiny microcomputer will be implanted into A's brain. This device will continuously scan all of A's brain activity and immediately transmit complete information about what it finds to a similarly small device, designed to receive its signals, which will be implanted into B's brain. This latter device will immediately encode onto B's brain the information received from the transmitter, just as it would have been encoded had it been acquired as the normal product of changes originating in B. As a consequence every psychological change encoded in A's brain (which will function normally throughout) is encoded almost instantly in B's brain and in virtually the same way as it was encoded in A's brain. Thus, throughout the time B is in a dreamless coma he will have a dispositional psychology exactly like A's of a few seconds in the past, but he will be completely unconscious and will not age physically. Except for the encoding in his (B's) brain, B will remain as John was just prior to his undergoing fission rejuvenation.

As it happens, fifty-five years after the procedure is performed A will die from an independently caused heart attack. As he draws his last breath the device implanted in his brain will send a signal to the device in B's brain that will cause B to wake up and begin a two-week-long recovery period similar to the one A had undergone. After B's recovery, he will leave the hospital, a *psychological* replica of A when A died and a *physical* replica of John when John was twenty years old. Once B is awake, he will age normally.

THE STRATEGIES OF IDENTIFICATION

I claim that it would be relatively easy to develop this example so that John's undergoing the fission rejuvenation procedure described in it is unquestionably a good deal for John (whether or not it would be a good deal for everyone). What it *means* to say that fission rejuvenation is a good deal for John is that given John's values, which we may suppose are both normal and healthy (though not the only normal, healthy values a person might have), and given John's circumstances and reasonable expectations, were John faced with the option of either undergoing fission rejuvenation or continuing normally, his better selfish choice (even though his prospects, without fission rejuvenation, are bright) would be to undergo fission rejuvenation.

What *makes* fission rejuvenation such a good deal for John is that by undergoing it he will secure a benefit as good (or, almost as good) for him as his doubling what would have been his remaining adult life span plus a benefit as good (or, almost as good) for him as his recovering physical youth in what otherwise would have been his old age. In other words, by undergoing fission rejuvenation John will be continued by A in pretty much the same ways and for the same length of time that without the procedure he would have survived as John; and then instead of John's dying when he would have died, he will be continued by B, thereby being continued in a physically youthful body, with a youthful life expectancy, just like the ones he had when he underwent the procedure, but without sacrificing A's psychological development or memories.

A crucial part of what makes it possible for John to secure such benefits is that by undergoing fission rejuvenation, he creates two fission descendants of himself with each of whom he can fully and rationally identify. This implies that John can anticipate (or quasi-anticipate) having the conscious experiences (and performing the actions) of each of his fission descendants pretty much as he would otherwise have anticipated having his own future conscious experiences (and performing his own future actions). What, in this example, facilitates John's fully identifying with each of his fission descendants is that prior to his undergoing fission rejuvenation, he knows, first, that only one of his fission descendants will be conscious at any given time; second, that the fission descendant who is conscious initially will cease to be conscious forever just as the other becomes conscious; third, that the causal mechanisms underlying the conscious experiences of whichever of his fission descendants is conscious at any given time are (initially) a proper subset of the same ones that redundantly underlie his (John's) own prefission experiences; fourth, that initially each of his fission descendants will have the same psychology that he had just before he lapsed into unconsciousness for the last time prior to his fission; and, fifth, that as long as his fission descendants are both alive, their dispositional psychologies will develop in tandem. I call these five features of fission rejuvenation the "strategies of identification." I shall explain below why they matter.

Extrinsic considerations, such as whether John thinks his fission descendants will be able to maintain his significant personal relationships and, more generally, whether he thinks they will be able to play the social roles that he now plays might also influence John's ability to identify with his fission descendants, as well as profoundly affect how good a deal John thinks that it would be for him to undergo fission rejuvenation. And were John to undergo fission rejuvenation, A's and B's extrinsic connections throughout their lives may profoundly affect how good a deal it actually was for John to have undergone fission rejuvenation. But since, in this example, there is no reason to think that A, at least, would have to have any trouble slipping neatly into all of John's social roles (John and A could keep it a secret that the procedure is performed), I shall not have much to say about these extrinsic considerations (for more on their importance, see White, 1989, and Rovane, 1990). For now it is enough to note that were fission rejuvenation inexpensive, reliable, and painless, it would be a good deal not only for John but for virtually any young person with normal, Western values who is in good physical and psychological shape and for whom, as I am supposing is the case with John, extrinsic considerations do not play a defeating role. Personally, I would give a lot to have been in John's position when I was twenty. Had I been in it (and had my current attitudes) I would have undergone fission rejuvenation gladly, without hesitation or reservations.

Parfit and others have appealed to fission examples to argue that there may be ways of continuing that are almost as good as ordinary survival. Even this relatively modest claim has been hotly contested. Fission rejuvenation, assuming it describes a procedure in which identity is lost, portrays an option that many people, I think, would prefer to persisting, even if their normal prospects, like John's in the example, were bright. That is one of the ways in which fission rejuvenation is superior to many other fission examples. Another way is that it is less vulnerable to attempts that philosophers, who on this issue are neoconservatives (granted, it is hard to think of David Lewis as a conservative), have made to show that identity really is what matters primarily in survival.

One might doubt whether fission rejuvenation does describe a procedure in which identity is lost. I shall deal with the main metaphysical motivation for this worry when I consider Lewis's views. I want now to consider the possibility that even though A and B, in the example, are physically separate and there is only a one-way causal influence between them, fission rejuvenation may not be a genuine case of fission. The source of this worry is that A's brain and B's brain do not develop independently of each other until after A's death. So, someone may think, A and B may simply be one person with two bodies and two brains.

To dispose of this worry I sketch two variations on fission rejuvenation that clearly are genuine cases of fission. In one of these B is awakened once a year for a few continuous hours and allowed to walk around the hospital grounds, thereby accumulating sensory input different from A's. On these once-yearly occasions B is asked whether he (still) thinks the procedure was a good idea (and, thereby, is treated by others as a separate person). Each year, B answers that he does still think it was a good idea, and, then, after a few hours of being awake he is put back to sleep. Everything else is as in the original example.

In another variation on the original example B remains unconscious until A dies, just as in the original example, but B processes the input he receives from A differently – say, in a slightly psychologically healthier way – than A processes it. So, for instance, bad memories of a variety of sorts (say, of personal rejection) that in spite of A's best efforts to counter their influence, detract from A's happiness, detract less from B's happiness. B does not forget the unpleasant incidents (he remembers everything A remembers), but his memories of them affect him somewhat differently. For instance, whereas these memories tend to embitter A, they do not tend to embitter B.

In these variations on the original example the two brains that emerge from the procedure are allowed to go out of synch just enough to quiet any doubts one might have about whether there has been genuine fission. While the details would have to be specified more fully to avoid problems of a variety of sorts, in principle I do not see any difficulty in doing this. I shall assume, then, that were someone to object to the uses to which I am going to put the original example, on the grounds that the procedure described in it does not induce genuine fission, I could make much the same points by appealing instead to one of these variations on it.

THREE VIEWS

I have claimed that the example of fission rejuvenation is invulnerable to recent neoconservative attempts to show that identity really is what matters in survival. I want now to test that claim.

Unger's View

Peter Unger's account of what matters in survival culminates in the following central claim on which almost all of his important conclusions depend: "No case that lacks strict survival will be as good as any case in which the original person himself really does survive" (1991, pp. 211–12). Unger is committed to accepting fission rejuvenation as a genuine case of fission and to accepting that a person does not persist through fission. He is, thus, committed to the idea that since John, in the example, has the option of continuing to lead a normally desirable life, it would be better for him to take that option and forego fission rejuvenation than to undergo it. As we have seen, fission rejuvenation seems to be John's better selfish choice. So, fission rejuvenation directly challenges Unger's central claim.

Unger distinguishes different senses of "what matters in survival." He intends that his central claim about the priority of identity should be understood only in what he calls his "prudential sense," which he says should be understood "in some such rough way as this":

> From the perspective of a person's concern for herself, or from a slight and rational extension of that perspective, what future being there is or, possibly which future beings there are, for whom the person rationally should be "intrinsically" concerned. Saying that this rational concern is "intrinsic" means, roughly, that, even apart from questions of whether or not he might advance the present person's projects, there is this rational concern for the welfare of the future being. So, in particular, this prudential use is to connect directly with our favorite sacrifice for future well-being test, namely, the avoidance of future great pain test. (1991, p. 94)

Unger thus defines his prudential sense of what matters in terms of what people rationally *ought* to be concerned about, not in terms of what people *actually are* or *rationally may become* concerned about. Thus, his central claim about the priority of identity, in its application to fission rejuvenation, is not directly about what people do or may prefer when faced with fission rejuvenation but, rather, about what they rationally ought to prefer and, ultimately, as we shall see, about whether they rationally ought to be willing to sacrifice as much now to protect their fission descendants from torture as to protect themselves from torture.

In the "avoidance of future great pain test," to which Unger referred, you are asked to imagine that it is you who is about to undergo whatever process, say, fission rejuvenation, is under discussion and that you have the following choices: You can experience a lesser, but still considerable pain now so as to ensure that the conscious being (or beings) who emerges from the process will experience no pain later; or, alternatively, you can experience no pain now and thereby ensure that the conscious being (or beings) who emerges later will "undergo really excruciating tortures for quite a long time" (1991, p. 29). To illustrate, Unger imagines that tomorrow he becomes a complete amnesiac with regard to his past life. Without personal memories, he concedes, "there will be quite a lot less" of what otherwise would have made his continued survival a desirable thing for him. Still, he insists, "even in this sad amnesia case there may be all of what [prudentially] matters." He knows this since "to spare myself from great electric shocks in two days time, I will rationally undergo just as many slight shocks now on the confident belief that I will become highly amnesiac, or at least very nearly as many, as I would on the equally confident belief that I will not become amnesiac" (p. 93).

In the fission rejuvenation example, John knows that without the procedure his prospects are good for a long and happy life. Yet, even on the assumption that John would not persist through the procedure, his opting for it could result in prospects for him that are even brighter. This is puzzling if identity is as important a prudential value as Unger says it is. Unger does not try to explain how such a puzzle might be resolved. On the assumption that identity is lost in fission rejuvenation, a reasonable resolution of the puzzle, as we shall see, is that identity is not as important a prudential value as Unger says that it is.

Suppose, for instance, that John confidently and rationally believed, first, that were he to opt not to undergo fission rejuvenation he would continue normally for many years and, second, that X is the highest number of slight shocks that it would be rational for him to experience now to spare himself the same number of really serious shocks a month hence. Suppose also that John confidently and rationally believed that were he to opt to undergo fission rejuvenation, then for quite some time after undergoing it, A would be his only conscious fission descendant.

On these suppositions, would it be rationally permissible, were John to undergo fission rejuvenation, for him to opt for experiencing X number of slight shocks now to spare A the same number of really serious shocks a month hence? Unger, if I understand him, would answer, "No, it would not be rationally permissible for John to undergo just as many slight shocks now to spare A as to spare himself the subsequent torture." Unger even suggests that it would not be rationally permissible for John to undergo just as many slight shocks now to spare both A that subsequent torture and also B a similar torture a month after B becomes conscious (1991, p. 263). However, Unger does not explain why, in his view, it would not be rationally permissible. Given what he says elsewhere, he would almost surely want to explain this by appealing to his idea that fission inevitably involves a serious enough "loss of focus" in the life of the person who fissions that under circumstances in which one's prospects are bright, fission is never prudentially preferable to persistence.

Unger never explains what he means by "loss of focus." Instead, he takes the notion as primitive and merely illustrates it in a variety of examples. For instance, he claims that it should be easy for us to appreciate that fission into a hundred descendants would seriously diminish "the focus" of our lives and that once we have appreciated this, it should then be easy for us to see that most of this loss of focus occurs even when we would fission into just two descendants (1991, p. 269). I agree with Unger that there is something to the loss of focus idea. Since he doesn't explain what he means by "loss of focus" it is hard to know whether what I have in mind is what he had in mind. In the forthcoming section on Sosa's view, I shall explain what I have in mind. Relying, for now, just on unexplained intuitions, it seems that whether or not any sort of loss of focus that has negative value is a problem either in old-fashioned fission examples or in the newer variations on them that Unger considers, none is a problem in the case of fission rejuvenation.

Unger briefly considers a few examples that raise problems for his view similar to those raised by fission rejuvenation. In the most relevant of these, his "no overlap case," he imagines that he undergoes a standard fission operation at the end of which one of his two fission descendants is superfrozen (and thereby rendered completely unconscious). This person is then kept frozen for fifty years, while the other fission descendant enjoys his normal active life as a philosopher. Unger further imagines that as soon as the philosopher dies, the super-frozen man is instantly super-thawed, after which he lives quite normally for another fifty years, enjoying his different career as an experimental psychologist (1991, p. 271; cf. Parfit, 1984, p.264). Unger says that in this case there would be more loss of focus than in normal persistence but less than in a standard fission scenario. He also says there would be less loss of focus than in his "day of overlap" case in which the impending psychologist is super-thawed "a day before the old philosopher's conscious life ends" (1991, p. 272). What, though, explains these comparative judgments?

The only explanation that Unger offers is that under certain circumstances fission branches may be "heavily discounted" and that when all but one is so discounted, then, even when a person has many fission descendants, there may be little loss in the focus of that person's life. Unger says that for someone with his own (Unger's) attitudes, a life with no conscious experience would not be "personally significant" and, hence, may be heavily discounted (1991, pp. 273–4). This suggests that, in his view, the main reason there is so little loss of focus in his no-overlap case is that both fission descendants are never conscious at the same time. However, Unger never explains why there is *any* loss of focus in his no-overlap case or why however much loss of focus he thinks there is necessarily affects how many slight shocks a person would be willing to endure to save his fission descendants from torture. Rather, he simply draws out for this example the implications required by his central claim.

Fission rejuvenation differs from Unger's no-overlap case in that when the second fission descendant becomes conscious, he takes up psychologically not where the donor left off but where the first fission descendant left off. Whether such a difference affects how much loss of focus there might be in such a case depends on what one means by "loss of focus." On Unger's account it is impossible to say. On the account I will provide it probably would affect it. It is clear, though, that whether or not Unger thinks this feature of fission rejuvenation would affect how much loss of focus there might be in fission rejuvenation, he would still think that a rational person ought to be willing to undergo more shocks now to spare himself from torture than to spare either one or both of his fission descendants from similar torture. However, to support this claim he has only unexplained intuitions.

As we saw in the preceding chapter, how many slight shocks a selfishly motivated person may rationally be willing to endure to spare a continuer torture surely ought to be heavily influenced by whether the selfish person can rationally anticipate (or quasi-anticipate) having that continuer's future painful experiences in pretty much the same ways that he would anticipate having his own future experiences. If the person can so anticipate having the future torture, it's hard to see why it should matter to him all that much whether he is the same person as the continuer of his who will later experience the torture.

In the fission rejuvenation example, the strategies of identification ensure that John would be able to anticipate having A's torture, at least if John's extrinsic relations to A also were to support his identifying with A. For instance, John would know that the physical mechanisms that would underlie A's experiencing torture, except for the elimination of redundancy, would be the same ones that would underlie his own future experiences were he to forego fission rejuvenation and continue normally. There is no reason why the elimination of redundant mechanisms, rationally would have to prevent John's conscious anticipation of having A's torture. After all, if John were to survive normally except for losing redundancy in

61

his brain this loss of redundancy would not have to prevent him from consciously anticipating having his own subsequent experiences. Thus, for John to be willing to endure as many slight shocks now to prevent A's torture as to prevent his own future torture surely would be rationally *permissible.* This result is all that's required to show that Unger's central claim is false. It is also all that's required to rebut his attack on the revolutionary idea.

Even though Unger's central claim is false, he deserves credit for having introduced the pain test, for it encourages us to distinguish importantly different questions that previous theorists sometimes failed to distinguish. For instance, in one of Unger's variations on his "basic case" he asks you to imagine that you are about to undergo a devastating surgical procedure as a result of which nothing of what is distinctive in your mental life (your memories, personality traits, character traits, capacities, views, interests, and so on) continues, but all of your core psychology continues. He further asks you to suppose that your core psychology flows on by the normal route of realization in your brain, that the person who emerges from this procedure has a capacity for conscious experience, and that the person who emerges has an IQ of about 30.

One question we can ask about your attitude toward this resultant person is whether you think this person is you. Another question – one that arises however you answered the preceding question – is whether, if these were your only choices, you would rather be continued by this person or simply cease and not be continued by anyone. And a third question is whether you think you could rationally anticipate having the experiences that this person would have. In my opinion, the great merit of Unger's pain test is that it highlights the possibility that even if you were to answer that the resulting person would not be you and that you would rather cease and not be continued at all than to be continued by this person, you still might think that you could rationally anticipate having the pain experiences this person would have, and, hence – even from what is arguably an egoistic perspective, or a perspective of self-concern – you still might be willing to endure a mild pain now to spare this person much greater pain later. In other words, Unger's pain test highlights the logical space between the question of whether a subsequent person is you and the question of whether you can rationally anticipate having that person's experiences.

What about the fact that philosophers get different results in applying the pain test to hypothetical puzzle cases? The problem, I think, is not with the pain test. Philosophers would get different results in applying any interesting intuitive test to the puzzle cases. How, though, should we respond to this fact? Surprisingly, at least to me, one of the most common responses has been for theorists to try to show that in spite of the differing ways in which philosophers actually respond to the puzzle cases, all of us should respond the same way. Parfit is in this tradition. He thinks he can show that all of us should value just psychological connections between ourselves now and people in the future. Unger too is in this tradition. He thinks he can show that all of us should value certain sorts of physical connections between ourselves now and people in the future.

Philosophers who try to establish such claims – in Chapter 1, I called them survival-value imperialists – will be able to dismiss some responses to the puzzle cases, which from the perspectives of their particular theories are unwelcome, on the grounds that these responses are obviously biased by some external circumstance or by some way in which the case has been improperly described. They will be able to dismiss other unwelcome responses on the grounds that the responses do not cohere with a person's responses to similar cases. But it is doubtful that such strategies will enable them to dismiss all such unwelcome responses or even to marginalize the ones they cannot so dismiss by showing them to be so rare that they can be discounted as aberrations. That is one of the main reasons why it is doubtful that the normative project of trying to show what should matter in survival should be at the focus of philosophers' concerns. I am not suggesting, as some have, that the fact that philosophers vary in the ways they respond to the puzzle cases means that we should dispense altogether with considering these cases. I agree with Parfit and Unger that the consideration of puzzle cases often provides valuable data. Rather, I'm suggesting that we may not be able to appeal plausibly to our responses to the puzzle cases (or to anything else) to justify any interesting version of survival-value imperialism.

A worthwhile question that would survive a shift away from the attempt to determine what should matter primarily in survival is that of determining what actually influences whether we identify with someone in the future. Personal identity/survival-value theorists have not entirely neglected this question. But most of them have put it on the back burner. Unger, for instance, has interesting things to say in response to it, but he is so preoccupied with specifying the conditions under which we *should* be prudentially concerned that related descriptive questions get short shrift. One might take the view that since the answer to this descriptive question has to be settled a posteriori, it should be settled by one of the empirical sciences. And social-psychologists have been on the borderline of this issue for decades. But it is unlikely that they (or any other empirical scientists) will address the question of explaining many of the identifications that most interest philosophers, for to do so they would have to consider how people who are sophisticated enough to understand all of what is involved in the infamous puzzle cases in the personal identity literature respond to these puzzle cases; and it is unlikely that social-psychologists will do that.

It would seem, then, that it is up to personal identity theorists themselves to bring the project of *descriptively* understanding the pattern of our (or at least their own) identifications to the forefront of our concerns. What's the alternative? Conceptual analysis in its application to personal identity and to what matters in survival has only limited interest. And the normative aspirations of survival-value imperialists are likely to continue to elude their grasp. So, it may now be time – perhaps well past time – for personal identity/survival-value theory to join the rest of philosophy of mind in becoming an a posteriori discipline, albeit one that relies for a crucial part of its empirical data not on the results of any science but on its own investigations.

Sosa's View

Ernest Sosa (1990) agrees with Unger that identity is lost in fission. In his defense of the traditional idea that identity is at least a precondition of what matters primarily in survival, Sosa distinguishes between what he calls, surviving, that is, persisting or continuing in a way that preserves one's identity, and what he calls, "surviving," that is, "extending causally into the future *with or without* branching." In discussing Sosa's views, I shall use the words *surviving* and *continuing,* respectively, to mark this same distinction. The heart of Sosa's defense of the traditional idea is his challenge to those who think that it is not surviving but only continuing that matters, to explain why branching does not diminish the value of continuing. Sosa argues that they will not be able to do this.

Sosa assumes that most of us, even if it were easy for us to massively fission-replicate ourselves, would not desire (or at least would not strongly desire) to produce as many replicas of ourselves as possible. He suggests, then, that the revolutionary proposal that identity is not what matters primarily in survival is probably just that "at the core of our egoistic concern lies rather the value of extending the causal influence of our psychology into the future *at least once.*" He asks, "Why not the more the better?" (1990, p. 309). In answering, he concedes that "one can have too much of a good thing." For instance, one can, even in a polygamous society, have too many spouses. But he claims that in cases of multiple fission replication in which oversupply is not a problem, most of us still would not strongly desire to replicate as many times as possible. He claims that while we can see the sorts of values that would be threatened, say, by having too many spouses, there seem to be no important values that would be threatened by having multiple fission descendants, except for the value of securing the survival of the mainstream protagonist (p. 311). In other words, his point is that while there must be a "defeating factor" to having multiple fission descendants, oversupply is not that factor, and the only other plausible defeating factor is loss of one's survival. He concludes that loss of one's survival is probably what explains why most of us would have so little interest in having multiple fission descendants.

Sosa claims, in addition, that the attempt to show that it is one's merely continuing (with or without branching) that matters puts one on a slippery slope: Any reason one could give why it is only continuing that matters would apply as well to the claim that it is only continuing minus the causal relatedness to earlier person-stages that matters, that is, that it is only there being future person-stages that matters. Hence, he concludes:

> We have found no train of reasoning for the return to more plausible desiderata except such as would carry us all the way to the original departure station, where what matters is one's full personal survival. And if this requires nonbranching, perhaps there is after all no plausible way to avoid this requirement. As far as we have been able to determine, no intermediate station offers coherent and stable refuge. (1990, p. 313)

In other words, identity *is* what matters primarily in survival.

In reply, I want to begin by conceding that for most of us the core of our egoistic survival values probably does consist, as Sosa puts it, "in extending the causal influence of our psychology into the future at least once" or, as I would put it, in having at least one continuer with whom we can fully (or at least sufficiently) and rationally identify. It seems to me that in comparison with that benefit, typically the benefits, if any, of having two or more fission descendants are minor. Of course, there are cases – fission rejuvenation is one – in which the benefits of having multiple fission descendants are major. But in all such cases of which I am aware, "extending into the future" more than once is desirable primarily as a means of ensuring that farther down the line, one extends into the future at least once. The question, then, is why most of us have so little interest in fission-replicating as many times as possible. In Sosa's way of putting this question, what is the defeating factor? Oversupply might *often* be the problem. For

65

instance, we might fear that fission descendants would compete with each other for our jobs or the affection of loved ones. Could oversupply *always* be the problem?

In a passage reminiscent of Unger's concern about loss of focus, Stephen White has suggested that the core problem with multiple fission replication is that it would interfere with many of "the external sources of access" that we normally have to a single future extension of ourselves (1989, p. 150). It would interfere, White thinks, because our knowing about our future behavior depends importantly on our knowing about "our future environment – the people to whom we have significant relations, the roles we play, the problems they present, and the opportunities they offer" – and, in a multiple-fission case, our environment "could never absorb the number of replicas in question." In such a case, White thinks, it would be hard for us to predict what the lives of our descendants would be like with anything like the same degree of assurance that most of us can predict our own future lives. So, he concludes, we could not "maintain the pattern of concern that characterizes our relations to our future selves for this many future extensions." He admits that if one were to fission into only two descendants, the loss in one's ability to predict and control them might not be significant. (So, he and Unger have somewhat different worries about the losses involved in fission.) But, he insists, in extreme cases of multiple fission the loss would be overwhelming.

While White has a point, it does not answer Sosa's challenge (nor, it should be noted, did White propose it to answer Sosa's challenge). Most of us, it seems, would have little interest in massive fission replication even if fission erased any memory of our having fissioned and even if each of our fission descendants were put into separate replica environments similar enough to our prefission environments that our normal external sources of access to future extensions of ourselves were kept intact. We would have little interest even though, in such cases of massive replication, life for each of our fission descendants would be just as predictable and controllable as our own future lives. Of course, unbeknownst to our fission descendants the loved ones they would interact with would not be our current loved ones but, rather, fission descendants of them. But to say that this is what would make such a future unattractive, or even radically diminish its interest, is in effect to say that loss of identity, that is, loss of (true) survival (at least in the cases of the identities of our loved ones), is the problem, not lack of external sources of access to our future behavior.

Why, then, would most of us not have more interest in massive fission replication? In my view, the basic reason is that to feel the sort of special concern for one's fission descendants that normally one would feel only for oneself, one has to be able to anticipate having the experiences (and performing the actions) that these fission descendants will subsequently have (and perform). And to do that one has to be able to project oneself into the psychologies of these fission descendants in pretty much the same ways that most of us currently project ourselves into what we imagine will be our own future psychologies. And as a matter of contingent fact, few of us can easily project ourselves into what we imagine will be the psychologies of more than one simultaneously conscious fission descendant. The often unpleasant and disorienting difficulty in trying to so project ourselves is immediately apparent in the case, say, of our trying to project ourselves into the psychologies of a hundred such fission descendants. But as Bernard Williams was the first to point out (and perhaps this is Unger's point), for most of us this difficulty can also be felt even in a case in which we would have only two simultaneously conscious fission descendants (Williams, 1970, pp. 177–8). Thus, this difficulty helps to explain why fission rejuvenation can be such an attractive option even though fission, say, into a hundred simultaneously conscious fission descendants, may hold little appeal.

In fission rejuvenation the strategies of identification remove all likely intrinsic obstacles to John's identifying fully and rationally with his fission descendants. That is why it may not be any more difficult for John to project himself fully into the one conscious psychology at a time that his fission descendants will have than it would be, were he to forego the procedure, to project himself into his own psychology in the future. And even if it were a little more difficult for John to project himself into B's conscious psychology because the transition from A to B would require adjustment to a youthful body, there is no reason why such a welcome adjustment "problem" should affect whether John is as rationally motivated to spare B subsequent torture as he would be to spare himself subsequent torture. After all, the prospect of a similar adjustment problem did not keep people from pursuing the fountain of youth.

As we have seen, when we anticipate having our own experiences in the future we do not merely expect that these experiences will occur to an appropriately causally related nonbranching continuer of ourselves. We also think of this continuer's experiences as *ours;* that is, we *appropriate* the experiences (in Chapters 5 and 6, I characterize the nature of this appropriation). Yet the best explanatory justification we can give for this act of appropriation is not that the continuer's future experiences are ours (that "explanation" is vacuous), but, rather, that the causal mechanisms that underlie our currently having experiences will persist continuously into the future and underlie our continuer's (and, hence, our own) future experiences. If this is a good reason to appropriate our own future experiences, that is, to anticipate not only that these experiences will occur but also our having them, then anyone in the future who satisfies this causal constraint (but not necessarily just such people; I. Persson, in correspondence; Clark, 1996) is a rationally permissible focus of our special egoistic concern, even if the person is one of many simultaneously conscious fission descendants. So, we may have as much *reason* to anticipate having the experiences of more than one simultaneously conscious fission descendent as we have to anticipate having our own future experiences.

Yet typically, most of us, I think, would have trouble actually anticipating having the experiences of more than one simultaneously conscious fission descendent, even if the causal mechanisms that underlie our currently having experiences were to persist continuously into the future and underlie the future experiences of our fission descendants. As we have seen, barring complications due to so-called extrinsic considerations, the difficulties that most of us would feel in trying to project ourselves into the psychologies of more than one simultaneously conscious fission descendent may not be based on there being rational obstacles to our doing so; rather, the difficulties would be due simply to limitations of our imaginative abilities. That, I claim, is largely why the prospect of having more than one simultaneously conscious fission descendent holds so little appeal. In sum, what I am suggesting is that the answer to Sosa's challenge is that in cases of massive fission replication, most of us experience limitations in our anticipatory imagination. These limitations are not a "defeater" in the same sense in which "oversupply," as in Sosa's spousal example, is a defeater; that is, our imaginative limitations do not imply that there is any value we have that is threatened by fission. Rather, these limitations merely prevent us from appreciating the positive value that potentially is in a case of fission. But even though these limitations are not a defeater, they are all that is required to make us indifferent to the prospect of fission into simultaneously conscious descendants. Hence, they are all that is required to answer Sosa's challenge.

What, then, of Sosa's slippery slope argument? The first problem with it is that it cuts both ways. It is doubtful that Sosa, or anyone, could give a non-question-begging justification for why survival (i.e., persisting normally) matters that did not apply equally to the value of continuing (with or without branching). The reason this is doubtful is that it would seem that the only sort of non-question-begging justification one could give for why survival matters would rely importantly on the idea that survival sustains the rational anticipation of having experiences and/or of performing actions; but the same could be said of continuing. In any case, Sosa does not try to give such a justification. So, until someone does give one that avoids this difficulty, apparently the same sort of slippery slope objection that Sosa says defeats the suggestion that it is continuing that matters applies equally to Sosa's own view that it is survival that matters.

The second problem with Sosa's argument is that his projected slide from our concerns extending to continuers all the way to their extending to causally unrelated future person-stages can perhaps be stopped. In the cases of both survival and continuing, the people whose future experiences (and actions) one anticipates having (and performing) are one's causal descendants. Thus, in undergoing some transformation, whether or not identity has been preserved, the causal mechanisms that underlie one's own experiences may, except for the elimination of redundancy, be the same ones that underlie the future experiences of one's causal descendants. In the different case of causally *unrelated* future person-stages, this reason for rationally anticipating having the experiences that these people in the future will have and/or of performing the actions they will perform cannot be given; and there may be no alternative justification.

In sum, in reply to Sosa, my suggestion is that at the core of our egoistic survival values is a desire to have (even if only through our fission descendants) a continuing opportunity to have experiences and to act. Initially, of course, we think this requires survival, and that is why survival seems so important. However, once we discover that whenever there is survival there is also continuing and that having the opportunities we crave requires only continuing, many of us may come to feel that survival per se is not so important.

Lewis's View

David Lewis (1976; 1983) has claimed that identity, as well as psychological connectedness and continuity, are what matter primarily in survival. In challenging the idea that identity is not what matters, Lewis relies on what I have called a "four-dimensional view" of persons. In my opinion, the main relevance *to the question of what matters in survival* of the switch from a three- to a four-dimensional view may simply be that on a four-dimensional view, one is not able to appeal to fission examples in the same way, if at all, to challenge the traditional idea that identity is what matters primarily in survival. That leaves open the possibility that there are nonfission examples that challenge the traditional idea. In Chapter 4, I argue that there are such examples.

The question I want to consider now is whether Lewis's latest, "postscript" argument for his view disposes of the challenge to the traditional idea posed even by fission examples (Lewis, 1983). I want briefly to indicate two reasons for being doubtful that it does. The reasons are, first, that his argument rests on a dubious assumption and, second, that even if this assumption is granted, the most that he can show by his argument is not that identity itself is what matters in survival, but that in fission examples the preservation of identity coincides with outcomes that also realize what matters in survival.

It would take us to far afield to summarize Lewis's entire postscript argument. For present purposes only a few things about it are crucial. One is that Lewis bases it on the assumption that since a prefission person-stage is a shared stage, any thought it has must also be shared. He understands this assumption to imply that if a prefission person-stage desires one thing on behalf of one of its fission descendants, then that very thought would also be a desire for the same thing on behalf of the other fission descendant. So, for instance, if a prefission person-stage of two people, C1 and C2, desires to survive, then that prefission person-stage cannot desire, say, that just C2 and not also C1 survives.

Lewis does not argue for this shared-desire assumption, which, as we shall see, is questionable. I concede, though, that if Lewis's shared-desire assumption is granted, then for the fission example he considers in his postscript argument, in which it is assumed that one of the people involved, C2, gets what he wants in survival, then Lewis can show that the other person, C1, who dies soon after the fission, also gets what he wants in survival. Lewis can show this since he can show that C1 could not want that he individually survive or that *both* fission descendants survive, but at most that at least one of the fission descendants survive; and, of course, one of the fission descendants, C2, does survive.

Yet even if this argument of Lewis's works for the fission example he considers, it is an open question whether it would work for some other fission examples. For instance, if the shared prefission person-stage of both C1 and C2 were a person like we have imagined John to be and he were faced not with the scenario Lewis sketches but, rather, with the prospect of undergoing fission rejuvenation, then that prefission person-stage would have had what Lewis calls "the strong plural desire" that *both* fission descendants survive. For in a failed attempt at fission rejuvenation, in which only one fission descendant (that lasts) is produced, it would be curious, at best, to say that every survival desire the person (or, shared person-stage) had who underwent the procedure was satisfied. After all, the reason that most people would undergo fission rejuvenation in the first place is to satisfy the strong plural desire. The prefission person-stage not only would have had such a desire; he also would have seen the satisfaction of his own survival values as depending on the different, but coordinated fates of each of the fission descendants (thus, apparently violating Lewis's shared-desire assumption).

Lewis *might* want to reply that in a case like fission rejuvenation, wanting to satisfy the strong plural desire is not part of what matters *in survival* to the person-stage contemplating fission. It is unclear, though, how he could establish this claim and also how important it would be even if he could establish it. For whatever we *call* the wants of someone who chooses to undergo fission rejuvenation, it seems clear that the person might be acting only for strongly self-interested reasons and yet still be acting primarily to fulfill the strong plural desire. It's hard, on Lewis's view, even to characterize what a person who chooses to undergo fission rejuvenation would be trying to accomplish.

Finally, even if Lewis can successfully dismiss all such reservations about his argument, it still seems that he has not shown that identity matters primarily in survival. For imagine that you are twenty years old (but with your current attitudes), in good physical and psychological shape, and deliberating about whether to undergo fission rejuvenation. Imagine also that you are uncertain as to whether a three- or four-dimensional view of persons is correct. How important would it be to you, in deciding whether to undergo fission rejuvenation, to determine which view of persons is correct? If you are like me, it would not be important at all. You would opt for fission rejuvenation even though you were unsure about whether undergoing it would sacrifice your identity. That strongly suggests that for such people – who, I think, would include many of us – persisting (identity) is not what actually matters primarily in survival. And I can think of no plausible reason for claiming that it should be what matters primarily.

THE BOTTOM LINE

Most of us do not want to die, at least not any time soon. Rather, we want a continuing opportunity, under at least minimally acceptable circumstances, to have experiences and to perform actions. Given available technology, we believe we cannot have such an opportunity unless we persist. Partly as a consequence of this, we value persisting, probably not in and of itself, but, rather, because we think it is a precondition of other things we value (Unger, 1991, pp. 212–17). And we are right to think this. Under the circumstances, identity (persistence) is a precondition of other things we value. That is partly why under the circumstances it is so important and also partly why it seems to be so important not only under the circumstances but also generally.

However, the supposition that there are ways of our continuing (or being continued) – fission, say, or other exotic possibilities – that might not preserve our identities but would, without too many unwanted side effects, allow us to fully and rationally anticipate having our continuers' experiences and performing their actions strongly suggests that for many of us identity is *not* nearly as important as it may have seemed that it was. I have suggested that many of us, if we had the chance, would opt for fission rejuvenation whether or not we thought it meant that we sacrificed our identities. If I am right about this, then, apparently, the most that many of us want primarily in survival is just to have continuers who have lives that are as advantaged as possible and whose experiences and actions we can fully and rationally anticipate having and performing. And in spite of the protestations of neoconservatives, there seems to be no reason to doubt that our wanting this could be rationally permissible. Thus, so far as the neoconservative objections we have surveyed are concerned, the revolutionary idea that for some – perhaps, for many – of us, identity is not what matters primarily in survival is secure. However, a caveat is required.

There may be an appeal to phenomenology, quite unlike any of the objections so far surveyed, on the basis of which one might question the revolutionary idea that identity is not what matters primarily in survival. This new objection will be based on the observation, first, that our "beliefs" about whether identity has been preserved through some transformation may occur on two "levels," one of which is theoretical and the other experiential, and, second, that the debate over what matters in survival has gotten off track in neglecting "experiential beliefs." In Chapter 6, I explain what I mean by this.

72

4

Transformation

We never vanish without a trace. Even in death, the stuff into which we decompose continues. Most of it is recomposed into other things, often things that are alive. We are food for worms. For those of us who want to continue, these facts are small comfort. Why exactly? For many of us, at least at the level of theoretical belief, it is not, I want to claim, because transformation is not good enough – because we want to preserve our identities; rather, it is because we do not identify fully with the things into which we expect to transform. If we were to identify fully with the people (or whatever) into which we expect to transform, many of us, as we shall see, would be happy to forfeit our identities provided we could secure certain other benefits.

Identity counts for something, so the value of these other benefits would have to outweigh the value of identity. But for many of us identity is not so valuable that it is difficult to think of benefits that might outweigh it. The trades many of us would be willing to make, and might rationally make, show, I think, that for many of us neither robust *physical* continuity nor robust *psychological* continuity either does or ought to matter primarily in survival. Whether the same nonfission examples can be used to show that not even minimal physical or psychological continuity matters primarily is a more difficult question.

MOST OF US WANT TO CHANGE

Voltaire once remarked, "It would indeed be very sweet to survive one's own self, to keep forever the most excellent part of one's being, while the other is destroyed" (1734/1937, ch. 6). The question I want to consider is whether, if it were possible to do this – that is, prior to bodily death to trade "up," even at the cost of our transforming into someone else – we would want to. I claim that under certain circumstances many of us would want to. That is, I claim that if we could choose what we would transform

73

into, many of us would actually prefer transformation to continuing as the persons we are.

Specifically, I claim that provided two conditions were met, many of us might prefer to transform so radically that as a consequence, according to criteria of personal identity to which many philosophers subscribe, we would cease and be replaced by others. The conditions are that we could fully identify with the persons into whom we would transform and that we believed that the other benefits to us of such a transformation outweighed the benefits of persisting. Finally, I claim that, in certain hypothetical circumstances, many of us rationally could satisfy these two conditions by choosing to transform into the (sorts of) persons we most want to be.

Two situations in which some would prefer to cease are not directly relevant to what I want to consider: First, if our options were very grim, many of us would prefer to cease than to continue; for instance, doomed to a life of continuously severe pain, many of us would prefer to die; and, second, under certain circumstances, a few of us who are very altruistic might choose to cease for the sake of others; that is, even if we had selfish options that were good, we might sacrifice our own good to promote the good of others. The circumstance I want to consider is one in which we are given a choice among alternatives that are at least as good as those among which we typically choose in our lives, and we choose just for our own sakes, that is, to promote selfish ends.

The person undergoing the fission procedure described in Chapter 1 donated half of his brain and all of his psychology to each of two fission descendants. Although he gave up a lot (a great deal of bodily continuity and perhaps also his identity), he did not give up everything. He was physically and psychologically continuous with both of his fission descendants. In opting for the procedure he bet the trade-off would be worth it. Probably most of us, in the same situation, would have made the same bet. But what happens if we raise the ante by asking the donor to give up more?

The key to unraveling our inflated estimates not only of the value of identity but also even of robust physical and/or psychological continuity is the innocent realization that most of us would rather change than stay the same, at least if we could choose the ways we would change. Probably you would like your body to be better than it is, perhaps stronger, more flexible, younger, more beautiful, and so on. Probably you would also like to be better psychologically than you are, perhaps more patient, generous, intelligent, knowledgeable, industrious, humorous, spontaneous, compassionate, or more (or less) something. Many would not want to change in ways that too radically disrupted their relations with family and close friends. But for some (say, for those without family and close friends or for those with family and friends who supported the change) this would not be a serious constraint.

I would like to change in all of the ways mentioned in the preceding paragraph. No doubt many others would as well. If I am right that many would like to change in all of the ways mentioned, then it is, I think, also likely that many would be willing to trade so many of their psychological and physical characteristics for better replacements that on the views of many (but not all) philosophers, their willingness to trade so much would amount to a willingness to cease; that is, they would have traded away too much to preserve their identities. This would show, on the assumption that one or another of these criteria of identity is correct, that for some of us identity is not what matters primarily in survival. I think it would also show this even if our only reason for not wanting to change in these ways is that it would interfere with our relations with family and friends. However, for the moment, I want to leave to one side this possible social complication.

Imagine, then, that it were possible for you to undergo a series of painless, safe, and inexpensive "operations" in each of which you would exchange some physical or psychological trait you have for a better replacement. So, for instance, you could, through a single, almost instantaneous procedure, one, say, that simply used sound waves and involved no cutting, become physically better – stronger, more flexible, more beautiful, and so on – or psychologically better – more patient, more generous, more intelligent, and so on. Without going into much detail about the specifics of the procedure, suppose that in any given procedure you could change only in relatively small increments and that no matter how many times you repeated the procedure, there would be recognizably human limits to the total amount you could eventually change along any given dimension. So, for instance, if you wanted to become physically stronger, you could increase your overall physical strength in any single operation only by about 5 percent of your current overall physical strength, and the most you could change along this dimension by repeating the procedure many times, at the minimum monthly intervals, would eventually make you about as physically strong as any current human. Imagine similar restrictions on the rate and extent of change along other dimensions. If such a procedure were available, many of us, no doubt, would continually improve ourselves through a series of such operations to the point where we would have significantly transformed ourselves. The benefits would be enormous. At last, a self-improvement program that works! How much would the benefits be worth?

Suppose that the only cost to you of undergoing such operations is that each time you underwent one, the memories you had of your life would fade somewhat, so that if you underwent the operation enough times, the memories you had of your life before the first such operation you underwent would fade entirely. Would the benefits be worth this price? Overall, as we grow older, our memories (especially of more recent events) tend to fade anyway, and in the scenario I am asking you to consider it would be possible to be reeducated about the past. So, for instance, before beginning the operations you could videotape yourself telling the story of your life, and then afterwards you (or your transformational descendant) could re-learn that story similarly to the way people learn from their parents of things they did as young children.

Some, no doubt, would not think the benefits of such an operation worth the costs. To them retaining their personal memories would be of overriding importance. Leibniz, for instance, once asked of what use it would be to a person to become king of China, on the condition that he forgot what he had been, and then suggested that it would be of no use since it would be the same as if God, at the same time he destroyed the person in question, created a king in China. However, in the scenario I am envisaging it would not be quite the same as that: The transformation would be in increments and you, not God, would have chosen it. In any case, imagine the details of my example fleshed out in a way that makes the operative procedures as attractive to you as possible. If such a procedure were available, would you choose to undergo it? I find, when I ask myself this question, that I would choose to undergo the procedure, probably many times.

Of course, the willingness of people to undergo such a procedure would vary drastically depending, among other things, on their current physical and psychological conditions and their current levels of self-acceptance. On the whole, a person who was old and unhealthy would have the greatest incentive to change; a person who was physically and psychologically very well off would have the least incentive. Given how much money affluent people currently spend on creams and ointments to reduce wrinkles and grow hair, as well as on cosmetic surgery, psycho-therapy, and so on (the list of so-called self-improvement programs and devices is all but endless), it is likely that if the procedure I have described were available, many people would be intensely interested, to say the least, in availing themselves of it.

Now change the example and imagine that while the operation is still safe, inexpensive, and painless, you can undergo it only once, but during that single operation you can change yourself as much as you like. Since you have only one chance at the operation and the alternative ways of changing yourself dramatically for the better are so onerous and unreliable, there would be a tremendous incentive to change yourself drastically, in fact, in all of the ways you would like to change so as to become the person you most want to be. Imagine that the incremental procedure has been in place for several years and that people generally, including the family and friends of those who underwent the procedure, as well as those who resulted from it, have been happy with the results.

In the new one-shot procedure, the greater the changes, the greater the tax on your personal memory (and also, perhaps, on your recognizability). You could change radically and become the (sort of) person you most want to be (assuming it would take a radical change for you to become that person) but only by ceasing to be either physically or psychologically closely continuous with your current self. On many theories of personal identity, perhaps on all them that weigh heavily the retaining of personal memories, this would mean you could change radically and transform into the person you most want to be only by ceasing to be the person you now are. For instance, if to become the person you most want to be you would have to transform into someone who was in effect an amnesiac with respect to your preoperative self, then, on robust-psychological-continuity accounts of identity the person who emerged from the operation would not be sufficiently psychologically continuous with your preoperative self to be the same person as you, and hence identity would be lost. Would you opt, nevertheless, for the operation?

Before deciding you would want to know much more about the procedure. For now, just imagine that these further details are such that the cost of the procedure is no greater than losing almost all of your personal memories and those of your physical and psychological traits you wish to change (thus greatly diminishing your physical and psychological continuity with your current self), and the benefit is transforming into the person you most want to be. If these were the costs and benefits, would you want to undergo the procedure? Can you imagine *any* way of filling out the details of the example so that you would? I can imagine ways of filling out the details so that I would. I suspect many others can for themselves as well. Once, for instance, in a talk to members of a philosophy club at an old age community, I described this procedure and asked how many of them, if the procedure were available, would want to undergo it. To my surprise virtually everyone in the club – about fifty people – opted enthusiastically and without hesitation for the procedure.

On theories of personal identity to which many philosophers subscribe, if you change abruptly so that the person who emerges from the change is neither physically nor psychologically closely connected to you, then that person is not you. Assume, for the sake of argument, that one or another of these theories is correct. How much would it matter to you that the changes you would want in the operative procedure just envisaged would cost you your identity (remember, we are setting aside, for the moment, possible social costs of having such an operation)? You can have the operation only once. You could choose to hold back from becoming (i.e., transforming into) the person you most want to be and only request such changes as are compatible with your remaining the person you now are. Or you could take the radical step of transforming into the person you most want to be.

I believe that I would take the radical step and that becoming the person I most want to be would require such drastic physical and psychological changes that the tax on my personal memory would be enormous and the physical and psychological connectedness to my current self so greatly diminished that on many theories of personal identity, the person who emerged probably would not be me. I also believe that in initiating the procedure I would be afraid, albeit irrationally. Yet I think I would choose the changes I want anyway, even if it meant I would lose my identity, *so long as I believed I could rationally anticipate having the experiences and performing the actions that my transformational descendant would have and perform.* I suspect that many others, even at the cost of their own identities, would make similar choices for themselves.

Occasionally philosophers have indicated that they might join such a group. William James, for instance, in concluding his classic account of the varieties of religious experience, remarked that he had not talked about immortality since to him "it seems a secondary point." He continued:

> If our ideals are only cared for in "eternity," I do not see why we might not be willing to resign their care to other hands than ours. Yet I sympathize with the urgent impulse to be present ourselves, and in the conflict of impulses, both of them so vague yet both of them noble, I know not how to decide. (1902, lec. 20)

In a similar vein Nicholas Rescher remarked, "It is not death we fear as much as meaninglessness and pointlessness . . . [W]hat ultimately counts for us is not so much the survival of our selves as the survival of our *values*" (1992–4, II, p. 150). Of course, unlike in the scenarios that James and Rescher probably had in mind, in the procedure under discussion it is not just that certain of our values survive, but that they are embodied in a person who we chose to transform into and with whom we fully and rationally identify. That should make the procedure under discussion a much more attractive option.

One might object that even if many people would rather become the persons they most want to be than retain their identities, this would not show that for these people becoming the persons they most want to be is what matters primarily to them in survival since these same people might even more strongly prefer becoming the persons they most want to be in ways that preserved their identities. I agree that most of us would prefer to change in ways that allowed us to retain our identities. However, this shows, at most, only that many of us would prefer both to retain our identities and to become the persons we most want to be, rather than just to become the persons we most want to be. If the question is which of these two matters most in survival, then we have to consider a situation in which we could have one of the two but not both. That is what we just did.

I think, though admittedly without proof, that in the sort of situation envisaged, where we could transform in the ways we would want to or else we could retain our identities but not do both, many of us would choose to transform. For those of us in this group, becoming the persons we most want to be, at least if we could fully and rationally identify with those people, matters more in survival than either robust physical or psychological continuity, even more, it seems, than identity.

MINIMALIST PHYSICAL-CONTINUITY THEORIES

The transformational examples just presented do not affect the views of certain minimalist physical-continuity theorists, such as Unger. He could reply that while the examples suggest that people might rationally choose to give up a great deal, they do not support the view that they might rationally choose to give up what is crucial: the physical mechanisms (or appropriately related descendants of them) that underlie a person's core psychology.

To answer such theorists, suppose, first, that while someone's brain is healthy, her body is ridden with cancer and her only hope for survival is to have her entire healthy brain transplanted intact to another healthy body. Suppose also that this transplantation procedure is perfectly safe. Finally, imagine that the body into which the donor's brain will be transplanted is better than her current body, not only in that it is healthy but also in many other respects that appeal to the donor. As Parfit has pointed out, the donor has not lost much if she jettisons her old body and moves her brain to the better body that awaits it. Such an operation would not be as bad as staying in the old body and dying of cancer, even if the death were painless. Vanity being what it is, if radical cosmetic surgery of this sort were available and safe, it is likely that many people would choose it, even if the old bodies they jettisoned were healthy. So, if physical continuity matters primarily in survival, it cannot be the continuity of the whole body but at most the continuity of the brain.

As Parfit has also pointed out, the importance of our brains, like that of our other organs (initially at least), is not intrinsic but derivative; that is, (initially) the brain's importance depends solely on the functions it serves. For most of us, if half of the brain were functionally equivalent to the whole, the preservation of our whole brain would not matter much in survival. And, it would seem, the continuity even of any part of the brain is not necessarily important. If some other organ, such as the liver, sustained our psychologies and our brains served the functions this other organ now serves, then this other organ would be as important in survival as the brain now is and the brain only as important as this other organ now is. So, it would seem that if something else – anything else – could sustain our psychologies as reliably as the brain, then the brain (i.e., the physical organ that actually now functions as the brain) would have little importance in survival, even if this other thing were not any part of our bodies (Parfit, 1984, pp. 284–5).

It is possible, though, that even though the importance of an organ is derivative and based solely on its being the vehicle for preserving a person's psychology, given that it has always been that vehicle, then the preservation of that organ matters importantly, perhaps even primarily, in survival. In other words, it is possible that even though something else might have assumed that organ's function of preserving a person's psychology and, hence, that under those imagined circumstances the organ that now serves that function would not have mattered importantly in survival, once an organ actually has served the function of preserving a person's psychology, then it does matter importantly in survival. But even though this is possible, it is doubtful that the very organ that has actually sustained your psychology, merely in virtue of its having sustained your psychology, thereby matters all that importantly to you in survival.

Imagine, for instance, that competent doctors discover that you have both a brain disease and a brain abnormality. The disease has not impaired the functioning of your brain yet. But if it is untreated, it will result in your death in the near future. Because of the abnormality, there is a simple, effective, and painless cure. The abnormality is that only one half of your brain, the half now diseased, has ever functioned. The other half has been lying dormant – healthy and perfectly capable of performing a whole brain's functions should the need arise, but nevertheless never functioning and not currently encoded with any of your psychology. There is a simple procedure the doctors can perform to switch the roles of the two halves of your brain: All of the encoded psychology on the diseased half of your brain will be transferred to the healthy half; as it is transferred, it will be erased from the diseased half and the healthy half will begin to function just as the diseased half did (and would have continued to function had it been healthy).

Suppose that the procedure is as quick and as simple (and as abrupt) as flipping a switch, that it will not affect subjective psychology, and that consciousness will be continuous throughout the procedure. Indeed, suppose that you (and the person who emerges from the procedure) will not even notice any change. Once the transfer is completed, almost instantaneously, the diseased half of your brain will become dormant and pose no further threat to your organism's physical or psychological health. In these imagined circumstances, how much would it matter to you that the half of your brain that has always sustained your psychology will no longer sustain it, while the half that has never sustained it will sustain it from now on? Probably not much. The procedure would not be as bad as death. Unless the procedure caused existential anxiety, it would not even be as bad as a root canal. So much for the derivative value of the organs that have actually sustained our psychologies.

Those who are skeptical of this response might imagine that whereas the procedure described is the simplest way of disabling the threat to the organism posed by the diseased half-brain, it is not the only way. An alternative procedure the doctors can perform is to repair your diseased half-brain through a series of twenty brain operations spread over the next twenty years of your life. Each operation will cost about one-half of your annual salary (suppose that insurance does not and probably never will cover the procedure) and will require two months of hospitalization. In addition, the operations will be disfiguring. When they are finally completed, you will be healthy enough, but your life will have been seriously disrupted and your body and face will be somewhat deformed. I assume that on your scale of values, the disruption, expense, and disfigurement, while bad, are not as bad as death. (If they are as bad as death, reduce their severity to the point where they are not *quite* as bad as death.) So, if the first procedure is as bad as death, then the second procedure is a better choice. Which procedure would you choose? I think most people would choose the first procedure.

How important is it as a feature of the example that the two halves of your brain are structurally isomorphic? Not much, I think. Change the example slightly so that now the doctors tell you that the underlying mechanisms by means of which the two halves of your brain would sustain your psychology are a little different. The doctors tell you that this difference makes your healthy half-brain a more efficient mechanism than your diseased half-brain (but not in ways that will affect your subjective psychology). You learn this is not just your doctors' opinion. Several noted brain physiologists who are following your case closely are unanimous in regarding this structural difference in your healthy half-brain as "a design improvement." Under these circumstances, I doubt that many people would object to activating the healthy half-brain for the reason that it is structurally different.

A physical-continuity theorist who feels that whatever organ has sustained your psychology must continue to do so to preserve what matters primarily in survival might object that, strictly speaking, the same organ – your brain – that sustained your psychology before the procedure will continue to sustain it afterwards, and so the example does not show that that organ does not matter importantly, much less primarily, in survival. Whether we would regard the two halves of such a brain as part of the same organ or as two different organs does not change the fact that what sustained your psychology before the procedure – just one half of your brain – will no longer sustain it afterwards.

To avoid this objection entirely, simply modify the example so that what the doctors discover is not that half of your brain is healthy – but, so far, nonfunctional – but, rather, that the two halves of your brain actually developed as separate organs. In other words, you have always had two (malformed) brains. One of your brains, the one that, so far, has been the sole sustainer of your psychology, is the one that is diseased. The other brain, the one that so far has never sustained your psychology and does not initially have any part of your psychology encoded on it, is just a healthy version of the diseased functioning brain, with or without some minor structural differences, as discussed earlier. The rest of the example goes as before and leads again to the same inevitable question: How much would it matter to you that if you allow the doctors to perform the procedure, the organ that has always sustained your psychology will no longer sustain it? The answer, I think, for most people, will be, not much.

Finally, a physical-continuity theorist, such as Unger, might object that what is important is the continuous existence of that part of the physically embedded structure of the brain (or whatever physical structure) that sustains the most basic parts of your psychology. This view is compatible with the idea that the actual organ might be replaced, provided the replacement is not too abrupt and provided enough of the crucial physical structure that underlies the most basic parts of your psychology remains continuously in existence. The organ replacement in my example was abrupt, and in one version of the example, there was structural change. Suppose, for the sake of argument, that the replacement was neither too abrupt nor the changes too drastic for the minimalist physical-continuity theorist.

Imagine once again that you are told that you must have a brain operation or else you will soon die and that there are two procedures available. In the first, physicians will record all of the information on your brain and, as they do so, break down those structures in your brain that sustain your psychology (turn them to "jelly," so to speak); then, just a few seconds later (or, in variations on this example, a few minutes, hours, or even days later), they will reconstruct your brain, including all of the structures they just erased, so that it is just like it was before, except that it will be rid of the disability that motivated the operation in the first place. In the second procedure, the physicians will subject you to a series of twenty brain operations spread over the next twenty years of your life, and so on, just as in the earlier example, with the same consequences and trade-offs. If the first procedure is as bad as death, the second procedure is a better choice. Which procedure would you choose? I think most people would choose the first procedure.

There are a host of other thought experiments relevant to the question of how much and in what ways physical continuity matters in survival. The result of considering them, I think, would be to show that it is relatively easy to imagine circumstances in which many of us would trade those aspects of our physical continuity that are said by various theorists to be essential to our identities for other benefits. Physical continuity matters, so we would not accept any old trade. It may even matter primarily that there is enough physical continuity that our transformational descendants are at least our descendants and, hence, not causally unrelated to us. But except possibly for that bare minimum of physical continuity, for most of us physical continuity does not matter primarily: It is always possible to imagine a trade that we would be willing to make. A critic might argue that our willingness to make such trades is irrational and hence shows nothing about what *should* matter in survival. So far as I am aware, no one has yet argued for this view. I think it would be difficult to argue for it plausibly.

For many people, radical transformation would have such disrupting negative consequences on relations with family and friends that it would not be worth it. What does this show? One thing, surely, it does not show is that in the case of *other* people not included in this group, identity is what matters primarily in survival. And there are people for whom such potentially disrupting consequences would not be a problem, perhaps because they don't have close personal relationships to others that would be disrupted by the consequences or because, for them, the consequences for such relationships would not, on balance, be negative.

In my view, there is a strong, self-deceptive tendency on the part of many people to exaggerate the degree to which they themselves are irreplaceable and, hence, to exaggerate the negative consequences on loved ones of their being replaced. In my opinion, in the cases of most of us, the truth of the matter − and not even necessarily the sad truth − is less flattering. It is that after a period of initial adjustment, which might not take long, the people who depend on us would get along just fine with improved replacements of ourselves, especially if we chose to have these replacements be disposed to love and care for them better than we now do. And, of course, hard as it may be for some of us to imagine, the replacements, by being *improved,* may well be *much* more understanding, *much* more helpful, *much* pleasanter to be around, and so on than we currently are and, hence, from the point of view of our loved ones, at least after an initial period of adjustment, even better than we are.

But aren't such motivations for wanting the transformation altruistic? What about our own egoistic points of view? Wouldn't we be losing a great deal to let our better replacements be the recipients of all this improvement in the quality of our personal relationships? In my view, it is hard to know in such cases where exactly to draw the line between egoism and altruism. Often we want improved relationships with those close to us not only for them but also for ourselves. So, in choosing changes that would lead to improvements in these relationships (or, in the descendants of these relationships), at the cost of our continuing, important benefits would accrue not just to our significant others but also to our transformational descendants. The question is, how much would it matter to us, from our so-called egoistic points of view, that it was these transformational descendants and not ourselves who would be the recipients of these benefits? In the case of many of us, it seems to me, there would be kinds of transformations and ways of bringing them about that would yield the answer, it wouldn't matter much. Yet this is not the right answer if identity were what matters primarily in survival.

MINIMALIST PSYCHOLOGICAL-CONTINUITY THEORIES

It is possible that the sort of transformation examples we have been considering do not defeat a minimalist psychological-continuity account of what *should* matter in survival. Richard Hanley has argued that this is indeed the case. In his view, for a choice to transform to be rational, the chooser has to intend to preserve certain pretransformation values. And this, he thinks, ensures that the chooser has to intend to preserve certain minimal psychological connections (1993).

The most difficult test for Hanley's claim is that of someone – John – who chooses to undergo psychosurgery in order to transform radically into a person with no desire to transform further; that is, John chooses to transform radically into a person who accepts himself just as he is. It would seem that, in so choosing, John may be choosing rationally to become the person he most wants to be; and yet, seemingly, the main values that motivate his desire to change are not values he wants to retain. Different versions of this example need to be distinguished.

In choosing to become a person with no desire to transform further, John, first, may want to transform into a person with certain of his psychological characteristics or, second, may want to transform into a person whose psychological characteristics (whatever they may be) are at least brought about in a certain way, say, by a progressively clearer understanding of reality. In each of these cases, Hanley says, John wants to preserve important parts of his psychology; for instance, in the second, John wants the survivor to be like himself in valuing truth.

However, contrary to Hanley, it is not clear, even in these two cases, that what John wants to preserve are important parts of *his* psychology. It depends on what the identity conditions are for psychological traits. As Persson has pointed out (in correspondence), it may be enough for John

85

that his "survivor" has values that are qualitatively identical to John's own. Rationality would not seem to require that John wants the survivor's values to be numerically identical to his own.

In any case, there is a more difficult version of the example for Hanley's claim. Suppose that John simply wants to become a person with no desire to transform further and that he doesn't care what are the other psychological characteristics of the person into whom he shall transform. Hanley concedes that, in this case, John's choice to transform might still be rational. After all, he says, it might be rational for someone with a strong sense of adventure to want to time travel even though he is ignorant of what that might involve. However, Hanley claims that it is doubtful whether on this third variation of the example John's choice to transform would reflect what matters to John *in survival*. In support of this idea he makes two distinctions.

First, Hanley claims that only in some cases in which one person is succeeded by another does the former person transform into the latter person; that is, not all successions are transformations. For instance, in his view, if one person were succeeded by another, but the two were causally unrelated, then the succession would not be a transformation. It seems to me that social context might in some cases replace appropriate causal relations in making what would otherwise be a mere succession a transformation (Kolak and Martin, 1987; Clark, 1996). But I agree that in the absence of any such context (and perhaps even in its presence), the example is best described as a succession rather than a transformation.

Second, Hanley claims that only in some cases in which a person transforms into another does the former person survive; that is, not all transformations are survivals. In support of this idea he provides an example in which a scientist has designed an artificial person who coincidentally is very like John. Before the scientist has a chance to push the button that will "start" his artificial person, John, in total ignorance of what is going on, accidentally pushes the button himself, thereby causing himself to end and the new person to begin. Hanley says that in such a case John does not transform into the new person even though John's ending and the new person's beginning are directly causally related. The reason, he says, is that John's ending and the new person's beginning are not appropriately causally related.

Hanley attempts to support this last claim by considering a spectrum of cases at one end of which are processes of transformation in which the person who transforms, John, clearly survives and at the other end of which are processes in which John clearly fails to survive. He says that in "moving back towards the nonsurvival end of the transformation spectrum," we pass through cases

> where John wants only to transform into a person who doesn't want to transform, as long as that person is not, e.g., lobotomized or otherwise mentally defective; where John wants only to transform into a person who doesn't want to transform, whatever their mental states; where John wants only to transform into a person, and doesn't care at all what values or states that person has; where John wants only to transform into a life-form, no matter what it is; and where John wants only to *transform,* no matter what the result. (1993, p. 216)

Hanley says – and in this I agree with him – that it is doubtful whether such cases are cases of survival, and hence it is doubtful whether they show anything about what matters in survival.

"It is just as plausible," Hanley says, "to describe such cases as showing what matters to John more than survival does" (1993, p. 217). However, in my view, once the notion of survival has been pried loose from that of identity, it is hard, in many cases, to say whether a transformation should count as a survival. The problem is not just that there are borderline cases but, rather, that it is unclear even what aspect of the seemingly clear cases it is that determines whether they are survivals. It seems to me that attempts to draw a line between such survivals and transformations inevitably devolve into trivial conceptual analysis. But if one abandons the idea that the distinction between transformations and survivals is an important one to maintain, what is one is to make of the idea that the values under consideration are those that matter to a person *in survival?*

Most of us want to persist; that is, we want to continue in ways that preserve our identities as the people we now are. We may want to persist partly for the sake of others. Almost certainly we also want to persist for our own sakes as well; that is, most of us want self-interestedly to persist. But what do we *really* want – that is, what do we want most fundamentally – when we want self-interestedly to persist? I claim that so far as our theoretical beliefs are concerned (as opposed to our experiential beliefs, to be discussed in Chapter 6), what most of us really want, so far as our so-called self-interested wants are concerned, is primarily to continue as (or to be continued by) some maximally advantaged being with whom we can fully and rationally identify. I call this claim the thesis that *continuing is primarily what matters* (in survival). Its main rival is the thesis that *persisting* (or, identity) *is primarily what matters.*

Admittedly, in real life, most of us most of the time want to persist and not merely to continue. The reason is that in real life our options are limited: To get what we want self-interestedly in survival we have to persist. That is primarily why, insofar as our so-called egoistic survival values are concerned, the preservation of identity seems to be so fundamentally important. However, were certain options available to us that are not available, then many of us could get what we want self-interestedly in survival merely by continuing. The evidence for this comes from expressed preferences in response to hypothetical forced-choice situations. As we have seen, it is not too difficult to show – on either a three- or a four-dimensional view of persons – that in certain hypothetical situations, continuing without persisting is for some people a more attractive option even than persisting in a normally desirable way. I do not say that in these hypothetical situations anyone rationally should want merely to continue rather than to persist. My claim is that, in these situations, for some people, first, it is rationally permissible to want self-interestedly merely to continue rather than to persist and, second, that this is in fact what some of us actually would want primarily.

Consider, for the moment, just such people; that is, consider just those who in some situations want self-interestedly and primarily merely to continue rather than to persist. The supposition that continuing is what matters primarily to them can explain *both* the preferences they reveal in certain hypothetical situations in which they would choose merely to continue *and also* those preferences they reveal in some hypothetical and in all actual situations in which they would choose to persist. By contrast, on the supposition that (in situations in which these same people superficially want to persist) what they *really* want is to persist, one cannot explain why they will in other hypothetical situations choose to continue rather than to persist, even when the option of persisting in a normally desirable way is available to them.

Thus, on the supposition that in situations in which these people superficially want to persist, what they really want is to persist, we need a plausible explanation of why these same people – in other situations in which they want merely to continue – change their minds about what they want. I cannot think of a plausible explanation for this. Hence, on the supposition that persisting is primarily what matters to these people, one must accept *as a basic unexplained datum* that in certain situations these people want to persist and in others they want merely to continue. That is why the supposition that to these people persisting is primarily what matters is both an ad hoc and a more complex explanation than the simpler, more generally applicable supposition that continuing is primarily what matters.

Consider, for instance, the sort of fission examples that have been centrally discussed in the personal identity literature. Those who are three-dimensionalists about persons think that people who fission into qualitatively identical fission descendants do not persist through the fission. Since it is relatively easy to construct forced-choice situations in which fission is one's best option even when there is a way of persisting that allows one to lead a normally desirable life, it is relatively easy to construct forced-choice situations in which it will seem to three-dimensionalists that continuing is a better option than persisting. Fission rejuvenation is such an example. For three-dimensionalists, on the supposition that *persisting* is what matters primarily, it is hard to explain peoples' preferences in such examples.

The usual response by three-dimensionalists who believe that persisting is (or is a precondition of) what matters primarily is to try to explain such examples away. The standard technique for doing this is, first, to direct attention to some supposedly overlooked aspect of the examples and, then, to claim that once that aspect of the examples is taken into account, persisting will be seen to be more attractive than continuing. Unger, for instance, uses this strategy when he draws attention to the negative value of so-called loss of focus, which he thinks inevitably occurs in standard fission examples. Sosa also uses this strategy when he argues that preferring continuing to persisting puts one on a slippery slope that leads inevitably to the view that being followed by a qualitatively similar, but causally unrelated "replica" is as good as persisting. As we have seen, these two ways of trying to explain away the troublesome examples do not work. I do not know of any other ways of trying to explain them away that work better.

Four-dimensionalists, on the other hand, think that in such examples the so-called person who chooses to fission persists through fission; that is, they think that identity is *not* lost since the prefission "person" is actually a shared person-stage of as many people as ultimately emerge from this and subsequent fissions (assuming, of course, that other relevant factors, such as psychological continuity, are preserved). Hence, on a four-dimensionalist view, fission examples, by themselves, cannot be used in the same easy way to show that what we really want when we want to persist is to continue. But on a four-dimensionalist view, there are alternative ways to use fission examples to show this, such as in the fission rejuvenation example. And depending on which unity relations among person-stages a four-dimensionalist thinks are necessary for personal persistence, there may be other, nonfission examples that can be used to show that continuing matters more than persistence. In the present chapter I have argued that there are such examples.

If I am right that there are such examples, one consequence is that for some people it is not persisting but, rather, continuing in certain ways that is fundamentally what matters in survival. But – and this is the issue raised by Hanley's criticism – in considering which ways are those certain ways, should we consider just ways of continuing that count also as ways of surviving or should we also consider ways of continuing that, arguably, do not count as ways of surviving? I would say, the latter. For if it is true that for some people it is not continuing in ways that count as surviving but rather simply continuing that matters, then that would be a significant fact about these people. It would not be so important that what matters to them is not what matters *in survival* if what matters to them in survival could be explained as a special case of some more basic sort of mattering.

The point, initially, of asking what matters in survival rather than simply asking what matters simpliciter was to exclude altruistic considerations. But in the kinds of examples we are considering now, it would seem that altruistic considerations have already been excluded. Assuming, then, that they have been excluded, the interesting question is not what matters primarily *in survival* – assuming we can make clear enough sense of the notion of survival to ask this question – but, rather, what matters simpliciter. The reason the latter is the more interesting question is that what we want to be able to do is to explain as fundamentally as possible our entire pattern of values. And determining what matters simpliciter rather than simply what matters in survival is our best way to do that.

Returning, then, to Hanley's main point, the question is whether it is a rational constraint on what we can choose to transform into that we choose to retain the values that motivated our choice to transform in the first place. As Hanley suggests, the answer may be yes, if the transformations at issue are only those that are also survivals and we can explain satisfactorily which transformations those are. But, how, other than by a trivial appeal to ordinary language, can we explain satisfactorily which transformations those are? And if we cannot nontrivially distinguish the transformations that are survivals from those that are not, and so allow – as relevant to the question of determining the rational constraints on what we can choose to transform into – only those transformation that are survivals, then, as I've argued, it is going to be much harder to show that it is a rational constraint on what we can choose to transform into that we choose to retain the values that motivated our choice to transform in the first place. Hanley has not explained how to distinguish nontrivially between those transformations that are and those that are not survivals. Hence, he has not shown that it is a rational constraint on what we can choose to transform into that we choose to retain the values that motivated our choice to transform in the first place. I cannot think of any better argument for that conclusion than the one he has given. Hence, I conclude that, so far as we know, it is not in general a rational constraint on our choices to transform that we choose to retain the values that motivated our choices in the first place.

I have argued that many people would rather transform into the persons they most want to be than they would to persist, provided they could fully and rationally identify with the persons they most want to be. In other words, under certain circumstances – not desperate circumstances but, rather, advantaged ones – many of us would prefer to transform into other people than to remain the same persons we are. And, I have argued, we would prefer this not for altruistic reasons but for selfish ones, or at least for reasons that are the motivational analogues of what in more familiar situations would count as selfish reasons.

This conclusion, I think, reveals something fundamental and perhaps also startling about our most basic so-called egoistic values. In simplest terms, it reveals that so far as our theoretical beliefs are concerned, many of us crave to be fulfilled more than we crave to be – that, paradoxically, if by choosing to cease to exist, we could realize our deepest "selfish" values, as in certain hypothetical circumstances it appears that we could, then we would choose to cease to exist.

Perhaps this result should not be so surprising. Many people, even now, choose to live shorter lives and/or to run grave risks of shortening their lives to realize selfish values. For instance, many people smoke cigarettes or drink alcohol merely because it pleases them to do so, even though they believe these practices probably will shorten their lives. Many athletes take steroids or other drugs to improve their performance even though they believe this practice probably will shorten their lives. Yet, in the central transformational examples considered in this chapter, life is neither lost nor shortened, nor even threatened. Only identity is lost. Death is a worse fate than the sort of loss of identity that occurs in these examples. Thus, the fact that many people would shorten their lives to realize selfish values, sometimes even rather trivial values, is evidence that many people – to realize their deepest "selfish" values – would choose to transform in ways that resulted in their ceasing to exist.

Finally, if I am right that we – many of us – crave to realize our deepest "selfish" values more than we crave to be, it is interesting to wonder what they – our transformational descendants – would crave. If this process of "trading up" were repeated over and over, through many cycles of "birth" and "rebirth," it would not be surprising if our deepest values, the ones that initiated the process in the first place, came to seem quaint. Perhaps the better selves that eventually emerged from this process would be more satisfied with themselves than most of us are with ourselves and would thus crave identity. A more exotic possibility – no more than a possibility, yet perhaps one worth thinking about – is that these better selves would grow weary of the cycle of birth and rebirth, of mere transformation into other selves, and crave a way of transforming that, while it involved sentience, took them beyond selfhood altogether.

5

Identification

Each of us identifies with himself in the past and in the future in a way in which normally we do not identify with anyone else. We identify with ourselves in the *past* primarily by remembering *having had* experiences and *having performed* actions. We identify with ourselves in the *future* primarily by anticipating *having* experiences and *performing* actions. Ordinarily we remember or anticipate having only *our own* experiences and performing only *our own* actions. That's because ordinarily our options include only those we have in real life.

As we have seen, there are hypothetical situations in which many of us would anticipate having the experiences and performing the actions of continuers of ourselves who, apparently, we do not think are ourselves and who, on many of the criteria of identity to which philosophers subscribe, are not ourselves; and we would anticipate having these experiences and performing these actions in pretty much the same ways we currently anticipate having our own experiences and performing our own actions. In other words, there are hypothetical situations in which, apparently, many of us have *identificatory surrogates*. As we have also seen, for those who are three-dimensionalists about persons the case that many of us have identificatory surrogates can be made by appeal to fission examples; but the case itself, whether it is being made for three- or for four-dimensionalists, does not depend on fission examples. It can be made without them.

In my view, if there is a great insight that has emerged from the last twenty-five years of debate over personal identity and so-called egoistic survival values, it is that, so far at least as our theoretical beliefs are concerned, in certain hypothetical situations many of us have, and apparently are rational in having, identificatory surrogates. This suggests that the distinction between self and other is not nearly as fundamental a distinction as traditionally has been thought. That is, if the insight is genuine, then, at least at the level of theoretical belief, our so-called egoistic survival values are, at bottom, not really egoistic at all but, rather, at most, "continueristic."

Of course, fundamentally, our so-called egoistic survival values may not even be continueristic, for it may not be a requirement of our having such identificatory surrogates that they be our causal descendants. But whether or not it is a requirement, the more important point is that if the insight is genuine, then at least at the level of theoretical belief, fundamentally, our so-called egoistic survival values are *at most* continueristic. For if, fundamentally, our values are at most continueristic, then, fundamentally, they are not really egoistic at all. And in that case, at the level of theoretical belief, the expressions of self-interest that all of us make, that both individually and socially are such an important part of our lives, would not fundamentally, but only relatively superficially, express our real values. That, if it is true, is an important fact about ourselves.

In the next chapter I want to explain why this insight, which is about what I am calling our "theoretical" beliefs, may not be the whole story about our survival values. However, if the insight in question needs to be qualified only for the reason I shall give, then for the purpose of our understanding the significance of the distinction between self and other, its needing to be qualified *only* for that reason will turn out to be as important an insight about ourselves as it would have been if there had been no need to qualify the original insight at all. In sum, in my view, either the insight is genuine or it is not genuine for an interesting and profound reason. Either way, we get a deep glimpse into the identificatory processes that underlie the ways we constitute ourselves.

What are the psychological processes involved in a person's having an identificatory surrogate? So far, neither philosophers nor psychologists have had much to say in answer to this question. The reason that philosophers have neglected it is primarily because it is an empirical question about our psychologies, and they have been preoccupied with normative and metaphysical issues. Ironically, in the past few decades philosophers of mind in general have taken a great interest in empirical questions, perhaps to the point where it would be true to say of philosophy of mind in general that it has become an a posteriori discipline. But philosophers of personal identity have not followed other philosophers of mind in this respect. The core philosophical discussion of personal identity has been almost wholly divorced from any sort of interest in genuinely empirical issues. The reason that psychologists have neglected investigating the psychological processes involved in a person's having an identificatory surrogate is that questions about these processes arise primarily in the context of thinking about how people respond to the puzzle cases in the personal identity literature; most psychologists are either unaware of these puzzle cases or professionally uninterested in them. Yet even though the psychology of our having identificatory surrogates has been neglected by theorists, it is difficult to see how one could *explain* the differing responses that philosophers give to the puzzle cases, which for three centuries now have been at the heart of their discussion of personal identity, without first going into it.

Consider, for instance, Parfit's notorious "branch line" example, in which he asks us to put ourselves imaginatively into the place of a person on Earth who is trying to teletransport to Mars (1984, pp. 200–1). In this example the person trying to teletransport succeeds in producing a replica of himself on Mars; but because the teletransporter malfunctions the person fails to dematerialize on Earth. Soon thereafter the person on Earth emerges from the teletransporter and is told believably that because his heart has been damaged he – the person on Earth – has only two more days to live. Parfit argues that he should not be too concerned since he ought to regard his replica's persistence – now taking place on Mars – as an adequate surrogate for what might have been his own persistence.

Whether or not Parfit is right about how the injured Earthling *ought* to feel, few philosophers who project themselves imaginatively into the position of the Earthling in this example *actually feel* as Parfit says they ought to feel; that is, few think that in the imagined circumstances they would actually regard the Martian replica as an identificatory surrogate for themselves. Why not? For those who are three-dimensionalists about persons, probably it is not because the Martian is an other. Most three-dimensionalists have already accepted that there are fission and spectrum examples in which they can identify in the appropriate way with others. For them something else blocks the identification. What? More fundamentally, what is the nature of the identification that in their cases is being blocked?

I want to suggest an answer to this more fundamental question. In doing so, I shall, for simplicity, focus just on the anticipation of having experiences. To avoid irrelevant distractions I shall consider just examples about which most of us would concede that the people in them who anticipate having the experiences under discussion are rational in anticipating having these experiences. I believe that an adequate, more general account of the psychological processes involved in surrogate-self-identification could be developed along the lines of the one I shall provide. This more general account would be applicable not only to the rational anticipation of having experiences, but also to that of performing actions, as well as to the remembrance of having had experiences and of having performed actions. I shall not provide this more general account.

On the account I shall provide, when we surrogately self-identify with someone in the future, who we anticipate will have certain experiences, we *appropriate* those experiences. This appropriation, which is usually a tacit but sometimes an explicit declaration of ownership, is not an isolated phenomenon that shows up only in the consideration of hypothetical examples; rather, it is at the heart of what psychologically binds us, individually, over time, as the persons we are. In other words, the element of appropriation that I want to explain is not just an ingredient of surrogate-self-identification but also of ordinary self-identification. It is what is left over when we delete from the process of ordinary self-identification that obtains when we anticipate having *our own* experiences and performing *our own* actions the (theoretical) belief that the experiences and actions anticipated are our own. And except for differences in its duration, this sort of appropriation is also an important ingredient in full-blown identificatory fantasies, such as occur when we identify fully with a character in a novel or a movie, or when as children we make believe we are someone else.

In contemplating hypothetical examples, when we appropriate future experiences we may do so not in a separate declaration of appropriation but, rather, by taking the person (or person-stage) whose experiences we anticipate having as the focus of what in normal circumstances would be self-regarding affective, cognitive, and behavioral dispositions. That is, assuming that in the imaginative projection of ourselves into hypothetical circumstances, most of us actually do have identificatory surrogates, I claim that our having them consists in our directing toward appropriate hypothetical others dispositions that in real life we also have but tend to direct only toward ourselves. Further, I claim that neither in real life nor in hypothetical circumstances do (or would) we direct these dispositions toward others who are neither ourselves nor appropriate surrogates for ourselves.

EMPATHY, SYMPATHY, AND IDENTIFICATION

There are a variety of ways that philosophers and psychologists distinguish between empathy and sympathy. As I understand the differences among empathy, sympathy, and surrogate-self-identification, empathy is one thing, normally sympathy is empathy plus something else (a kind of super-empathy), and normally surrogate-self-identification is sympathy plus

96

something else (a kind of super-sympathy). The something else that when added to empathy makes it sympathy has to do with adopting the objectives of the other with whom one is empathic. The something else that when added to sympathy makes it surrogate-self-identification is what I am calling "appropriation." Since I am going to be concerned with surrogate-self-identification just insofar as it involves the anticipation of having experiences, in this restricted focus the something else that when added to sympathy makes it surrogate-self-identification is a certain sort of appropriation of another's future experiences.

When I say that *normally* sympathy includes empathy and *normally* surrogate-self-identification includes sympathy, I intend to allow for the possibility that sometimes they do not. In the case of surrogate-self-identification, in particular, there are times when it occurs without including empathy in the way I am going to define empathy. This happens partly because our lives, especially in those aspects of them that become routine, can make us somewhat numb to our own experiences. Thus, as we shall see, there are cases in which we may surrogately self-identify with ourselves but without also empathizing with ourselves.

To be empathic, in my use of the term *empathy*, one must understand a situation from another's point of view. To do that, one must imaginatively, yet more or less realistically, represent to oneself how things look or feel to the other. By "how things look" I mean how things are perceived, that is, what sorts of visual, tactile, auditory, gustatory, olfactory, or kinesthetic sensations the other has; by "how things feel" I mean what sorts of emotions or affect another experiences. By "another" I mean either another person, another sentient being, or else oneself in the past or future (thus, veridical first-person memory, in my view, is a special case of empathy).

Such a representation of how things look and/or feel to an other may be, but does not have to be, experiential. If the other, say, is in an embarrassing situation, then to be empathic with her embarrassment one must understand from her – the embarrassed person's – point of view *that* the situation is embarrassing. Depending on the circumstances this may require that one understand either what in the situation she consciously thinks is embarrassing or, alternatively, what actually is embarrassing. Being empathic always requires that to some extent one represent to oneself the other's feelings; minimally one must at least know that the other has certain feelings and also something of their character. But the representation can be "thin"; in particular, it does not require that the empathic person shares in the other's feelings, say, by actually being embarrassed himself.

Sometimes people use the word *empathy* to mean only *affective empathy*. I am using the term more broadly to include also what is sometimes called "cognitive empathy." In empathic encounters a common causal chain goes from cognition of the other's state to affective empathy, to sympathy, to action. In my view, it is important to distinguish two different sorts of cognition that may initiate such a chain. Nonempathic cognition does not require that you understand the other's state or situation from the other's point of view. Empathic cognition does. So, whatever sort of cognition may initiate such a causal chain, at some point empathic cognition has to enter into it, perhaps as an ingredient of affective empathy. But neither cognitive nor affective empathy requires that the empathic person adopt the other's objectives. For instance, if the other is in distress, even the robustly empathic person may not feel any urge to help. Thus, being empathic – even robustly empathic – is compatible with being sadistic. Being robustly empathic might even heighten sadistic pleasure.

Sympathy requires more. To be sympathetic with another, one must not only be empathic with the other but also adopt at least some of the other's (relevant) objectives. For instance, if embarrassment causes someone to want to remove herself from an embarrassing situation, then, all else being equal, a sympathetic person will both want that the embarrassed person be removed from the situation and also be disposed to help her accomplish that objective. Typically, a sympathetic person will not just understand *that* the other has some feeling, say, is embarrassed, but also share in the other's feelings, say, be embarrassed *for* the other. When the sympathetic person does share in the other's feelings, this sharing helps to explain why the sympathetic person is motivated to adopt some of the other's objectives. I say that typically, rather than always, a sympathetic person will share in the other's feelings. This is to leave open the possibility that there is an unattractively cerebral form of sympathy – we could call it "Kantian sympathy" – that does not involve sharing in the other's feelings and, hence, that derives its motivation to help the other from a different source, say, respect for "the moral law."

Surrogate-self-identification, on the other hand, requires even more than is required by sympathy. It requires, at the minimum, that a person relate psychologically to the other's experiences and actions almost as if they were the identifier's own. In the case of future experiences, say, it requires that you would adopt pretty much the same constellation of attitudes and behavioral responses toward the person who will have the future experiences, and toward the experiences themselves, that ordinarily you would adopt only toward yourself in the future, and only toward your own experiences.

In the next chapter, I shall suggest that in addition to adopting certain attitudes and behavioral dispositions, surrogate-self-identification may also involve the identifier's structuring her experience in a certain way, namely, in a way that phenomenologically creates a distinction among the contents of her experience between "the observer," that is, herself, and "the observed." In this chapter I shall ignore this complication.

The initial task, then, in giving content to the notion of surrogate-self-identification, is to characterize the attitudinal and behavioral responses associated with (or constituitive of) it. I assume that these responses are not just occurrent but also dispositional. Since I think my explanation of what is included in these attitudinal and behavioral dispositions is more than some will be willing to admit is included, I want to begin by critiquing a variety of less complicated proposals, beginning with ones that give relatively thin accounts of surrogate-self-identification and, then, building up, step by step, to those that view it as a thicker phenomenon. My hope is that by understanding why each of these earlier proposals is too thin the reader will understand why a thicker proposal, ultimately why my proposal, is needed.

ALTERNATIVE PROPOSALS

1. *Weak Psychological Connection:* A person (or person-stage), S surrogately self-identifies with some person (or person-stage), S*, who S believes will exist in the future, just if S believes that S is (or soon will be) strongly psychologically connected to S* (cf. Rovane, 1990).

(For the sake of brevity, in subsequent proposals, please read, "S, surrogately self-identifies with S*," as short for, "a person [or person-stage], S, surrogately self-identifies with someone [or some person-stage], S*, who S believes will exist in the future.")

Objection to 1. Suppose the injured Earthling, in Parfit's branch-line example, passionately wants to spend his last two days with the woman of his (and his replica's) dreams. Suppose further that although the Earthling and his replica both want to spend these two days with this woman, only one of them gets to do it and it is up to the Earthling to decide which one. On the most natural ways of elaborating this example, if the Earthling were to chose to let his replica spend the two days with this woman, his choice would be not only other-regarding in the trivial sense that he would be putting someone else's interests ahead of his own, but it would also be genuinely altruistic. The Earthling's replica is not only another person but one whose experiences, if the Earthling is like most of us, he would not anticipate *having*. That's why the Earthling would not equate his interests with his replica's interests. It is also why it would be extremely odd if the Earthling's foregoing the desired experiences so that his replica could have them were to seem to him self-interestedly to be just like – or even almost as good as – his having the experiences himself.

2. *Moderate Psychological Connection:* S surrogately self-identifies with S★ just if S believes, first, that S is (or soon will be) psychologically connected to S★ and, second, that S★ will be S's causal descendant (i.e., a causal descendant of S's *current* person-stage).

This hypothesis avoids the problem with the preceding one since part of the reason it seems so plausible that the *injured* Earthling does not anticipate having his replica's experiences is that he does not believe his replica is a causal descendant of his current person-stage. Just prior to attempting to teletransport, when the Earthling did believe his replica would be a causal descendant of his (then) current person-stage, he did anticipate having his replica's experiences. However, once he emerged from the teletransporter and realized that his replica already existed on Mars, he ceased to anticipate having his replica's experiences.

Objection. Had the Earthling, just prior to attempting to teletransport, expected what was actually going to happen, his identification with his injured causal descendant on Earth, who he probably would have thought would be his closest continuer, may well have prevented him from surrogately self-identifying with his Martian replica. But in that case he would have failed to surrogately self-identify with his Martian replica even though he believed both that he would soon be psychologically connected to his Martian replica and that his Martian replica would soon be his causal descendant.

3. *Strong Psychological Connection:* S surrogately self-identifies with S★ just if S believes (i) that S is (or soon will be) psychologically connected to S★, (ii) that S★ is (or soon will be) S's causal descendant, and (ii) that S will cease before S★ begins.

Objection 1. In teletransportation examples, even under these three conditions, many do not anticipate having the experiences of their teletransported replicas and, hence, do not surrogately self-identify with them. So, surrogate-self-identification cannot consist just in meeting these three conditions.

Objection 2. Under these three conditions, many who consider fission examples in which they cease and are replaced by two simultaneously conscious fission descendants do not anticipate having the experiences of both of (or even of either of) their fission descendants and, hence, do not surrogately self-identify with them (Williams, 1970, pp. 177–80).

Summary

The basic problem with all three versions of the psychological connection thesis is that each focuses on how a person *believes* she is related to her replicas but without also taking into account how the person *feels* about being related to the replicas in those ways. But feelings, and not just their associated beliefs, are an important determinant of whether a person surrogately self-identifies.

4. *Equal Value:* S surrogately self-identifies with S$\star$ just if S values S$\star$ (or S$\star$'s interests) as much as S values S (or S's interests) (Jencks, 1990, p. 54; Mansbridge, 1990, p. 14; see also Eisenberg, 1982, pp. 339–59).

Objection. A person who sacrifices himself heroically for another – say, who throws himself on a hand grenade to save his buddies – may at the moment he chooses to sacrifice himself value the interests of those others as much as or even more than he values his own interests, and yet he still may not anticipate having their experiences. In surrogate-self-identification what matters is not just the purely quantitative question of *how much* one values the interests of others, but also the qualitative consideration of *how* one values those interests.

5. *Thin Experiential Empathy:* S surrogately self-identifies with S$\star$ just if S imagines S's (or S$\star$'s) experiencing from S$\star$'s perspective (Perry, 1976, pp. 75–6).

6. *Thick Experiential Empathy:* S surrogately self-identifies with S$\star$ just if S vividly and spontaneously imagines S's (or S$\star$'s) experiencing from S$\star$'s perspective (I. Persson, correspondence).

Objection 1 to Proposals 5 and 6. Every night people go to bed (dispositionally) anticipating having the experience of brushing their teeth in the morning. Yet they rarely, if ever, vividly or spontaneously imagine, from anyone's perspective, that experience. This is not because their anticipation of brushing their teeth tends to be dispositional rather than occurrent. It is because their experience of brushing their teeth tends to be boring. If those who dispositionally anticipate having the experience of brushing their teeth were occurrently to anticipate having this experience, most of them still would not vividly and spontaneously imagine having it, even from their own perspectives. Rather, they would just cognitively register that the event of their brushing their teeth was going to occur.

If brushing one's teeth was more exciting, then when people occurrently anticipated brushing their teeth they would be more likely to imagine vividly and spontaneously having the experience. But even then it would not necessarily happen. Some people are not very good at feeling (even) their own lives. As it is, for most people brushing their teeth is a humdrum experience and their anticipation of it is more cerebral than sensual. Thus, while proposals 5 and 6 may specify a sufficient condition for surrogate-self-identification they do not also specify a necessary one.

Objection 2 to Proposals 5 and 6. Add to the ways I earlier developed the branch-line example the supposition that the injured Earthling, while he is contemplating whether to let his replica rather than himself have the experiences they both desire, discovers that he (the Earthling) is frequently caused to have jealous feelings by vivid and spontaneous images he has of what it would be like, from the perspective of his replica, for his replica to make love with the woman of their dreams. Of course, the images that the Earthling imagines are also in all *internal* ways what it would be like, from his own perspective, for him to make love with this woman. Even so, in his visual fantasies of his replica and the woman there are *external* clues – the fantastic wall paper, the green Martian haze outside the window – that remind the Earthling that his fantasies are of his replica's experiences and not his own. To the Earthling this makes all the difference. He wants it to be him and not his replica who experiences making love to this woman. So, when the Earthling vividly and spontaneously imagines what he takes to be his replica's experiences, he feels jealous.

We may think the Earthling's jealousy is silly. Perhaps it is. But the scenario just sketched is nevertheless a possible one. And there would be nothing irrational about the Earthling's jealousy – nothing, that is, any more irrational about his jealousy than most of the more mundane sexual jealousies that each of us has occasionally experienced. The important point is that although the Earthling's having the vivid and spontaneous images mentioned of what his replica's experiences would be like arouses his jealousy, it does not ensure that he anticipates having his replica's experiences. If it did ensure this, he would not have been *bothered* jealously by these images, or if he was, it would have been irrational for him to have been bothered jealously by them.

Summary

One basic problem with both of the empathy theses under consideration is that they claim to provide necessary and sufficient conditions of surrogate-self-identification. The most they can claim plausibly is to provide a sufficient condition. Another basic problem is that even if they claimed just to provide a sufficient condition, they focus on empathy rather than on sympathy. As we have seen, even vividly and spontaneously imagining another's experiences from the other's perspective does not ensure that you adopt the other's objectives. And your not adopting the other's objectives may cause you to fail to surrogately self-identify with the other.

7. *Thin Sympathy:* S surrogately self-identifies with S★ if S vividly and spontaneously imagines S's (or S★'s) experiencing from S★'s perspective and also adopts *some of* S★'s (relevant) objectives as if they were S's own objectives.

Objection. This proposal leaves open the possibility that one will appropriate future experiences of one's own that are going on at the same time as those of the person with whom one is sympathetically connected, thus giving one a strong motive not to anticipate *having* the other's experiences.

Consider, first, an example of this in which there is no fission: Velma is extremely *sympathetic* with her children, particularly when it comes to their suffering. She believes that in two days, on Friday, when her children go to the dentist, they will suffer horribly. Bothered by this prospect she often vividly and spontaneously imagines from her childrens' perspectives the painful experiences she believes they will have. In addition, she adopts her childrens' (relevant) objectives as if they were her own objectives; all else being equal, Velma is disposed to help her children avoid the pain they are scheduled to endure. But, alas, all else is not equal. Velma believes that to remain healthy her children need to go to the dentist. So, she makes them go.

As it happens, Velma not only empathically anticipates the painful experiences her children will have on Friday, but she also anticipates having, on Friday, her own empathic experiences of her childrens' concurrent suffering. She expects that these future empathic experiences *of hers* will be painful, but she thinks that qualitatively they are likely to be somewhat different from *her childrens'* concurrent painful experiences. Her thinking this strongly suggests that in Velma's anticipating having these empathic experiences of her own, she is not anticipating having her childrens' concurrent painful experiences. As it happens Velma does not anticipate having her childrens' experiences. If asked why she does not, she would reply that she does not anticipate having her childrens' experiences because she is not them.

Now change the example slightly: Suppose that everything is as before except that Velma knows that on the morning of the day before her children go to the dentist, that is, on Thursday, she will fission into two replicas of herself, each of whom, when they originate, will be qualitatively identical to herself. The person-stage of Velma that fissions, as it fissions, will simultaneously dematerialize. One of the replicas, Velma★, will remain conscious throughout the next few days. The other, Velma★★, will spend the entire time in a coma.

Suppose that Velma is a three-dimensionalist about persons and, so, believes that fission undermines identity and hence that she, Velma★, and Velma★★ are each different people. Under these circumstances, if Velma were again, on Wednesday, to say of the suffering her children will experience two days hence at the hands of the dentist, "I don't anticipate having their (her children's) experiences since I'm not them," we might well reply: "Ah, but you do anticipate having Velma★'s painful empathic experiences, don't you, even though you're not Velma★? So, perhaps you are mistaken in thinking that you don't anticipate having your childrens' painful experiences."

Suppose Velma responds, "Yes, I do anticipate having Velma★'s painful empathic experiences even though I'm not Velma★, but that's because the very same causal mechanisms that now underlie my current experiences will underlie Velma★'s experiences. I do not anticipate having my childrens' painful experiences because these same causal mechanisms will not underlie their experiences." This sensible response would express Velma's quite understandable tendency to appropriate only her close-enough-

104

than-which-none-are-closer continuers' experiences (cf. Nozick, 1981, ch. 1). The fact that her reply is sensible shows, first, that thin sympathy is not enough for surrogate-self-identification and, second, that the reason it is not enough is not (or, not just) that the person with whom one identifies may be another person.

8. *Thick Sympathy:* S surrogately self-identifies with S⋆ if S vividly and spontaneously imagines S's (or S⋆'s) experiencing from S⋆'s perspective and S adopts *all* of S⋆'s objectives as if they were S's own.

It may seem that the problem with the thin sympathy proposal is that it leaves the would-be surrogate-self-identifier with too much psychological autonomy. In the case of Velma, for instance, it allows her to have objectives that conflict with her childrens' objectives. The current proposal closes this gap.

Objection. This strengthening of the sympathy proposal does not solve the basic problem with the thin sympathy proposal. That problem was not that Velma did not share all of her childrens' objectives but, rather, that she could satisfy the requirements of that proposal and yet not believe that *any* experiences that *she* (or any of her fission descendants) will have *while* her children are having the experiences she anticipates *they* will have are qualitatively identical with *their* experiences. So long as Velma believes this, it would prevent her from anticipating having her children's experiences even if she were to adopt all of their objectives.

Summary

A basic difficulty with the sympathy proposals under discussion is that neither attends sufficiently to the ways in which S's beliefs about the qualitative differences between S's own future experiences and other concurrent experiences can affect the pattern of S's identifications. For instance, Velma believes, quite understandably, that she cannot anticipate having both her own experiences and her childrens' concurrent and qualitatively different experiences; since Velma does anticipate having her own (or Velma⋆'s) experiences, then this belief of hers prevents her from anticipating having those of her children.

9. *Thick Copy-Sympathy:* S surrogately self-identifies with S⋆ if (i) S vividly and spontaneously imagines experiencing from S⋆'s perspec-

tive, (ii) S believes that the experiences S will have that are concurrent with those S⋆ will have are qualitatively identical, and (iii) S adopts all of S⋆'s (relevant) objectives as if they were S's own.

This proposal seems to avoid the problem with the preceding one. If, in the first Velma example, the requirements of this proposal had been satisfied, then Velma would have believed that the experiences she and her children would be having concurrently, while her children were experiencing pain from their visit to the dentist, would be qualitatively identical. And so Velma would not have had the same motive as before for distinguishing between her and her childrens' concurrent experiences.

Objection. But Velma may have a different motive for distinguishing between them. It is not enough that Velma believes that the experiences she will have while her children suffer are *qualitatively* identical to the concurrent experiences of one or another, or both, of her children. For Velma might believe that and yet still believe that her experiences and her childrens' experiences are *numerically* different, in which case Velma would not be anticipating having her childrens' experiences but only experiences that were qualitatively identical with her childrens' experiences.

10. *Thick Identity-Sympathy:* S surrogately self-identifies with S⋆ if (i) S vividly and spontaneously imagines S (or S⋆) experiencing from S⋆'s perspective, (ii) S believes the experiences that S and S⋆ will be having simultaneously are numerically identical, and (iii) S adopts all of S⋆'s (relevant) objectives as if they were S's own.

Objection. It is not clear what is involved in S's belief that S's future experiences will be numerically identical with S⋆'s. So, it is difficult to evaluate this thesis. On one interpretation of what such a belief might involve, the belief is implicit in certain dispositions that S has toward S⋆, and, hence, depending on which dispositions these are (an account of some of them will be provided shortly), S's belief may well constitute appropriation of S⋆'s experiences. S's belief might also be such that it involves explicit appropriation of S⋆'s experiences. Since it is unclear what S's belief would involve, it is clearer to leave the notion of belief out of the formulation of the proposal.

APPROPRIATION

11. *Appropriation:* S surrogately self-identifies with S⋆ *just if* S either explicitly or implicitly appropriates S⋆'s experiences.

I shall explain what appropriation involves in a moment. First, I want to do away with the suspicion some might have that this proposal cannot be right since, if it were, philosophers or psychologists would already have noticed the element of appropriation. The fact is that many have noticed.

Locke, for instance, had appropriation in mind when he remarked that "where-ever a Man finds, what he calls *himself,* there I think another may say is the same *Person.* It is a Forensick Term, appropriating Actions and their Merit" (*Essay,* 1694/1975, II, ch. 27, sec. 26; p. 346; see also the quotations from Locke in the Introduction). Rousseau had appropriation in mind when he remarked that a psychological process he had undergone "was to nourish myself on situations which had interested me in my readings, recalling them, varying them, combining them, appropriating them to myself so much that I became one of the characters I imagined" (Rousseau, 1969, I, pt. 1). But it was William James who came closest to getting the kind of appropriation that I want to discuss clearly into view. In trying to be sympathetic with Hume's basic insights yet still do justice to the evident fact that we do experience ourselves as selves, James remarked that "each thought is thus born an owner, and dies owned, transmitting whatever it realized as its Self to its own later proprietor." It is, James continued, "this trick which the nascent thought has of immediately taking up the expiring thought and 'adopting' it, which is the foundation of the appropriation of most of the remoter constituents of the self. Who owns the last self owns the self before the last, for what possesses the possessor possesses the possessed" (1890, I, pp. 371–2).

Each of these remarks, and others that might have been cited, captures something of what I want to say about appropriation. None of them gets it quite right. For instance, in the case of James's remarks, it is not the thought that does the appropriating but rather the person (or the person's brain) who has the thought. And whereas James and the others suggest that the appropriation is explicit, usually it is expressed only implicitly in a variety of dispositions. On the relatively rare occasions when the appropriation is explicit, the person may actually declare that he anticipates having the other's experiences (or, more commonly, that he remembers having had them). As we shall see, poignant examples of this occur in the literature on multiple personality disorder. Failure to notice that the act of appropriation generally is implicit may have kept James from suggesting an account of the dispositions in which it is expressed. I want now to suggest an account of these dispositions.

When the act of appropriation is implicit, at least three elements are centrally involved: first, people who do the appropriating experience *affect* of some sort that normally they would experience only when anticipating their own future experiences; second, they *cognitively contextualize* the anticipated experiences similarly to the way ordinarily they cognitively contextualize only their own future experiences; and, third, they *behave* as if the future experiences were their own. For instance, if someone, S, were anticipating having the experience of winning the Nobel Prize for literature (i.e., the experience of actually being presented with the prize), probably (i) S would feel not only pride but a certain self-satisfied delight (affect) at having written the prize-worthy works, (ii) S subsequently would narratize the history of S's life differently and, thereby, change her understanding of the meaning or significance of many previous aspects of her life (cognitive contextualizing), and (iii) S would exhibit related behavioral symptoms of having appropriated the imagined experience – for instance, S subsequently might adopt a grander tone in professional correspondence or plan vacations differently (behavior).

Each of these appropriative dispositions admits of degree. Each could be explained more fully. The list of them could be extended. It is unclear, however, whether instantiation of these sorts of dispositions is what someone's appropriating future experiences she does not believe are her own consists in and, hence, whether instantiation of them is what surrogate-self-identification consists in or whether these dispositions are a symptom of something deeper. I believe (but cannot prove) that they are a symptom of something deeper and also that there is an experiential symptom of this deeper condition. (The fact that there is this experiential phenomenon – by the way, whether or not it is a symptom of something deeper – can be used to answer the objection to the earlier empathy proposals that is based on the muted character of the anticipation of humdrum experiences, such as the experience of brushing one's teeth.) In the next chapter, I discuss this experiential symptom.

Whatever the full story of surrogate-self-identification, it is clear that ordinarily when one appropriates anticipated experiences one does so without explicitly declaring ownership of the experiences. Rather, one simply responds in a variety of distinctive ways to the prospect of these experiences happening, including the affective, cognitive, and behavioral ways mentioned. Although the details of how people so respond are likely to vary from person to person and with the same person over time, the responses that people make are ones that ordinarily they do and/or would make only to what they thought were going to be their own future experiences. Saying just what these responses are is a complicated project. I do not pretend to give more than the beginnings of an account. (However, I claim that there are some such distinctive ways in which people so respond and that these include the three elements of affect, contextualization, and behavior mentioned.) My account will be limited in another way as well. I shall not go into the question of how the identification of future experiences fits into the larger complex of identificatory processes that collectively figure so importantly in constituting selves. For the most part philosophers have ignored these identificatory processes. This neglect is puzzling since mention of them often surfaces near the heart of an important philosophical thesis that is widely discussed.

Harry Frankfurt, for instance, in a well-known paper on freedom of the will, touched briefly, but revealingly, on such identificatory processes when he characterized a "wanton" as someone who does not prefer that some, rather than other, of his first-order desires should constitute his will and, thus, "has no identity apart from his first-order desires." Frankfurt contrasts such a person with an unwilling addict who "identifies himself" through "the formation of a second-order volition with one rather than with the other of his conflicting first-order desires." Frankfurt says that, in so identifying himself, the unwilling addict makes one of his conflicting first-order desires "more truly his own," withdrawing "himself from the other." This, in turn, Frankfurt says, gives the unwilling addict a basis for saying that "the force moving him to take the drug is a force other than his own, and that it is not of his own free will but rather against his will that this force moves him to take it" (1971, pp. 12–13; see also, Sacks, 1995, pp. 101–3). However, neither Frankfurt nor others, so far as I know, have had much to say about what such identificatory processes are or how they work.

To me it seems obvious that such identificatory processes, while involving a different sort of identification from surrogate-self-identification, are intimately related to surrogate-self-identification. However, except for pointing out that these other identificatory processes exist and have been neglected by philosophers, I shall not go into the question of how the different sorts of identificatory processes that collectively contribute to constituting the self are related. Clearly, providing such an account would be a large undertaking. Equally clearly, the aspect of identificatory processes that I am going to discuss, important as I think it is, is merely the tip of an iceberg. My hope is that my account will encourage others to explore what lies beneath the surface. Before giving my account, I want, first, to reply to a way in which someone unsympathetic to my initial proposal might try to nip it in the bud.

Objection. Consider the case of a Pavlovian-conditioned dog who after hearing a bell, seemingly enters into an anticipatory state of expecting the experience of eating a meal. Does the dog anticipate *having* this experience? It is hard to say. One possibility is that the dog does not anticipate at all but, rather, just salivates, gets excited, perhaps even empathically imagines, from the inside, the experience of eating a meal. In spite of such behaviors, the dog may lack the conceptual repertoire he needs to anticipate either *his* having the experience or even *his continuer's* having the experience. The dog's cognitive state may stand to the genuine human anticipation of having an experience much like emotional contagion – so-called animal empathy – stands to genuine human empathy (see Martin and Barresi, 1995, pp. 479–81). A second possibility is that the dog does not anticipate *having* the experience of eating the meal, but does anticipate *that* the experience of eating it will occur, and his anticipating this, which would presumably require less conceptual sophistication than would be required by his anticipating his having the experience, is what explains why he salivates, gets excited, and so on. Finally, a third possibility is that the dog does anticipate either *his having* the experience or simply *having* the experience and that his anticipating this involves appropriation (albeit of a more primitive sort than I am going to suggest is the characteristic way that humans anticipate having an experience). None of these three possibilities would be a problem for the position I want to defend. It would be a problem – were it not just a theoretical possibility but also one that we had some reason to think actually obtains – were the dog genuinely to anticipate having the experience of eating the meal but without any appropriation. However, there is no reason to think this possibility obtains.

Consider, though, a related example, based on one due to I. Persson (in correspondence), in which a person is so heavily conditioned to expect a meal after he hears a bell that if there were to be a few negative instances (i.e., a bell but then no meal), he would still upon hearing the bell enter into an anticipatory state that is more or less as vivid as the one he experienced before the negative instances. Suppose, further, that somehow you have been hooked up to this person throughout his conditioning so that you experience his sensations of hearing the bell and tasting the food as vividly as you experience your own sensations. As a consequence, when this person hears the bell and enters into an anticipatory state of expecting the meal, you enter into a very similar anticipatory state. Finally, suppose you know that you have just been disconnected from this person and that, after being disconnected, if you were asked either whether you believe that

110

if this person were given a meal you would experience his sensations as he eats it or if the bell were to ring you would be given a meal, you would reply sincerely that you do not believe either of these things. Yet when you hear the bell you enter into an anticipatory state similar to ones you entered into prior to the disconnection.

Someone might suggest that since under these circumstances you do not now believe you are going to get the meal after you hear the bell, you do not own or appropriate the future experience of eating the meal; in fact, since you believe you will not have that experience you might even explicitly disown it. Yet it may seem that when you hear the bell, you still anticipate having the experience of eating the meal. Doesn't this show, then, that all that is required to anticipate having an experience is vivid and spontaneous imagining, from the inside, of what the experience would be like? And if that is all that is required, then appropriation is not also required.

Reply. There are two difficulties with this objection. One is that in the example your apparent anticipatory state after being disconnected and hearing the bell may not be genuine. It may, rather, be like the first of the possible scenarios sketched earlier in the case of the dog: The dog has various experiences and exhibits various behaviors not because he thinks a meal is imminent but for other reasons.

The other difficulty is that, in the example, your apparent anticipatory state may actually involve appropriation; for instance, while part of you – the part that controls your speech mechanisms – may not believe you will get the meal, another part of you may. (In the next chapter, I explore a way in which this possibility might be realized.) This other part of you – the part that believes you will get the meal – might include, but not necessarily be limited to, the conditioned mechanisms that trigger your anticipatory state. To put the point crudely, there is no reason to think that in the example you are "of one mind." Perhaps the part of you that believes after being disconnected and hearing the bell that a meal is on the way has appropriated the imagined experience of eating the meal. In that case, the example poses no problem for my view.

Return to the example of someone – say, you – anticipating having the experience of winning the Nobel Prize. Suppose, as was the case with Bertrand Russell, that you are a candidate for the prize mainly due to the lucidity of your philosophical prose. Suppose that you anticipate having the experience of winning. Whatever the full account of your anticipation,

111

unless you are quite unusual (in ways other than the ones that contribute to making you a candidate for the prize) your anticipating having the experience of winning would differ from your empathically anticipating *my* experience of winning. It would differ not just because our internal perspectives are different – recall the Martian jealousy example – or just because we are different people but, rather, for other reasons as well. I do not think these other reasons, whatever exactly they are, *necessarily* prevent you from anticipating having my experiences. But if you are a normal person, then they will as a *matter of fact* prevent you from anticipating having my experiences.

For instance, so far as affect is concerned, unless you are a Mother Theresa type, you would not look forward with the same emotion to the experience of watching me win the prize as you would to having the experience of winning it yourself. Even if we were great friends and you were thrilled that I won the prize, phenomenologically your thrill almost surely would not be the same as one you would feel if it were you who was going to win it. We do not have a good vocabulary for thrills, so it is hard to say just how the two would be different. But ordinarily no one is going to confuse the feeling expressed by, "Damn, I can't believe I really won the prize," with that expressed by, "Damn, I can't believe you really won it." Of the two feelings, only something like the former feeling would be appropriate to the anticipation of *having* the experience of winning the prize.

My suggestion, then, is that we can understand the affect component of what is distinctive about surrogate-self-identification in terms of a distinction (as in Figure 1) between those *affective* dispositions that normally would accompany narrowly self-interested choices, which I want now to call "self-regarding affective" dispositions, and a different set of affective dispositions that I shall call "other-regarding." The distinction between cognitive and affective dispositions, roughly speaking, is that between what a person thinks and what a person feels.

For instance, imagine someone who sincerely claims – perhaps under the influence of Hume or the Buddha – to have given up her belief in her own continuing identity. Generally, in spite of what such a person may say she believes, her self-regarding *affective* dispositions will continue to operate in a normal way. In other words, even though she might sincerely deny that there is a continuing person with whom she is identical and might even back up this denial in a rationally sophisticated way, her underlying affective dispositions may well be – indeed, almost certainly would be – pretty much the same as those of people who have more normal beliefs.

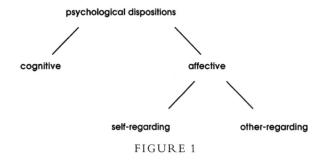

FIGURE 1

For instance, if such a person thought that her body was going to be tortured mercilessly tomorrow, she would be terrified in the same way and to the same degree as she would be if she thought that she would be tortured mercilessly tomorrow. Speaking roughly again, we might say that what such a person thinks about her lack of identity with any future person is merely cerebral – an affair of the head, but not of the heart.

Typically this sort of psychological and behavioral dissociation can be expected whenever a person adopts theories that cut too drastically against his natural beliefs. Yet even though the belief of a Humean or a Buddhist that she is not identical to any future person may be a thin, theoretical veneer on her underlying cognitive and affective dispositions, it cannot *simply* be dismissed as something she self-deceptively thinks she believes but does not really believe. For she may understand clearly that some of her theoretical, cognitive dispositions are out of sync with many of her other cognitive and affective dispositions. And if she does understand this, then she is not, as would be typical in a case of self-deception, failing to draw an unwelcome conclusion from evidence for it that should be obvious to her. On the contrary, she may have a heightened and, because heightened, especially painful awareness of her predicament.

There are analogous dissociations. A skeptic about self is a lot like an epistemological skeptic who, in spite of what he says he believes, continues to make practical choices and to respond emotionally in a normal way. Such a skeptic typically will treat some propositions he claims not to have reason to believe the same ways that normal people treat propositions they claim to know (for instance, he exits buildings via their doors rather than their second-story windows) and other propositions the same ways that normal people treat propositions they claim not to know. He may or may not be self-deceived. And the same can be said of the person who, in some of the puzzling examples in the personal identity literature, apparently chooses selfishly to sacrifice her own existence to bring another into existence who she does not believe, even at some deeper level, is herself. Such examples illustrate the difference between theoretical cognitive dispositions to believe or to say one believes, on the one hand, and affective dispositions to feel certain ways one would feel if one did believe, on the other.

There are more subtle distinctions that could be drawn among affective dispositions. Consider, for instance, what might be called "emotional beliefs," such as my fear of a snake that I know is not dangerous or my fear of falling, in circumstances in which I know I won't fall, such as when I press my nose up against the window in the viewing room at the top of the World Trade Center. In such cases, do I believe, on some level, that the snake is dangerous or that I will fall, or do I merely react emotionally as if I have these beliefs, even though I do not have them? It is hard to say. And for present purposes it is not important to decide. However, even if it were true that I have the beliefs, it would seem that I have them less robustly than an epistemological skeptic typically would have the normal belief, which he claims he has no reason whatsoever to think is true, that it is safer to exit a building from a door than from a second-story window. Perhaps, then, we should not think of beliefs as something people either have or lack simpliciter but, rather, as something they have (or lack) to certain degrees or in certain ways. For present purposes I shall ignore such complications.

So far as affective dispositions themselves are concerned, both self- and other-regarding affective dispositions, whether or not they include a belief component, are *primarily* concerned with feelings. Our task is to determine which distinctively *self*-regarding affective dispositions might naturally extend to a person's close-enough-continuer-than-which-none-is-closer even if, for theoretical reasons, the person believes this continuer is another. There are, no doubt, many. For present purposes, it will suffice to mention two: "affective anticipations" and "unconditional giving." For clarity, I shall (as in Figure 2) contrast the latter disposition with an *other*-regarding affective disposition to feel that the person for whom one sacrifices is in one's debt and, hence, to expect an expression of gratitude.

There are two crucial differences between self- and other-regarding affective anticipations. First, self-regarding affective anticipations are a person's dispositions to *feel* the way normally he would feel as a consequence of anticipating *his* having specific kinds of experiences in the future. But, as we have seen, in some of the puzzling examples in the personal identity

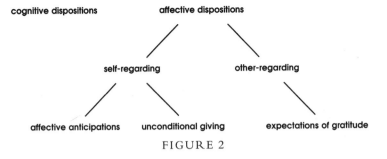

cognitive dispositions   affective dispositions

self-regarding   other-regarding

affective anticipations   unconditional giving   expectations of gratitude

FIGURE 2

literature, anticipating having the experiences of one's continuers might *feel* the same as anticipating having one's own experiences even though one believes these continuers are others. All that is necessary for this to happen is that a person's self-regarding affective anticipations take the person's continuers as their objects. For instance, contemplating a fission procedure, the donor may be convinced for theoretical reasons that neither of his fission descendants will be the same person as himself, yet still *feel* the same (or almost the same) in anticipating the experiences of one or the other, or both, of these fission descendants as the donor would feel in anticipating his own experiences.

If the donor knew, say, that his fission descendants would be tortured mercilessly tomorrow, he might be terrified, whereas probably he would feel only pity if he knew that someone else (i.e., someone with whom he did not surrogately self-identify) was going to be tortured. In other words, it might *feel* to the donor as if the torture that is going to happen to the fission descendants was going to happen to him. For instance, a person might feel that regardless of whether his personal identity is preserved through some transformation, so long as certain other continuities are preserved, such as his psychology and perhaps even his bodily form, then the resulting person, whether or not that person is him, is an appropriate object of his self-regarding affective dispositions. Joseph Priestly, for instance, in remarks of his to be discussed in the next chapter, expressed some such view.

The other crucial difference that I want to discuss between self- and other-regarding affective dispositions is the presence or absence of the feeling that someone for whom one sacrifices is in one's debt. Normally, the disposition to have this feeling will be present when we sacrifice for someone else but not when we sacrifice for ourselves. Hence, the disposition I am calling, "unconditional giving," will be among our *self*-regarding

115

affective dispositions, whereas its opposite, "expectations of gratitude," will be among our *other*-regarding ones.

What I have in mind is that people who sacrifice to promote their own future welfare will almost never feel that they are in their own debt. That is, people will not, as a consequence of their sacrificing now to promote their welfare in the future, care whether in the future they ever express gratitude, or indeed any good feeling, to their "past selves" for their having sacrificed; and such people will not later have a feeling of *resentment* occasioned by their failing to express gratitude to their past selves or even by their failing to like their past selves. But people who sacrifice to promote the welfare of others almost always either will feel that the person for whom they have sacrificed is in their debt or at least that as a consequence of their having sacrificed, the other should have a positive feeling toward them.

If, say, a soldier throws himself on a hand grenade to save his buddies and then lives to discover that his buddies are not sufficiently appreciative, probably he will resent their not giving him, as he might put it, "the credit he deserves." Parents who sacrifice for their children and later come to feel that their children are not sufficiently appreciative may also feel resentful, or at least be disappointed, that their children do not have more positive feelings toward them. This familiar disposition extends even to trivial and automatic cases of self-sacrifice. For instance, if you were to notice that the stranger who just vacated your table in a coffee shop left his book and you rushed down the sidewalk to return it to him, probably you would feel slighted if he took the book without expressing gratitude or at least some positive feeling toward you.

The point I am making is not conceptual but empirical. It is, first, that our sacrificing for others tends to cause us to have certain feelings – most easily detected when the expectation of gratitude that our sacrificing engenders has been flouted – unlike any feelings that normally would be caused in us by our sacrificing for ourselves, and, second, that these feelings have no close analogue in any normal feelings we have toward ourselves. I deny, for instance, that there is any normal feeling we have that when the sacrifice is for others, is called "expecting gratitude," but when it is for ourselves is called something else, say, "expecting to feel thankful." I concede that theoretically we could "expect gratitude" from ourselves and that, in unusual cases, this may happen. My claim is that if it happens at all, it is rare. I cannot prove this – although the lack of symptoms in our speech or behavior of any such feeling directed toward ourselves is evidence for my view.

In other words, what I am trying to isolate is an experience of "emotional calculation" that is almost never present in our sacrifices for ourselves but almost always present in our sacrifices for others, even for others as emotionally and genetically close to us as our own children. My claim is that when this calculation is made, normative expectations are generated that, if flouted, usually cause resentment; and if, at the time a person makes a sacrifice, she contemplates the *real* possibility that the beneficiary of her sacrifice will not be appreciative when an expression of appreciation would be appropriate, she will probably experience, even then, some resentment in anticipation of her possibly having a fuller experience of resentment later.

Narrowly self-interested sacrificing, on the other hand, is relatively unburdened with such normative expectations. We sacrifice freely for ourselves, without thinking about or even caring whether we will look back and feel grateful; it is enough that we will enjoy the advantages intended to flow from our sacrifices. In this respect, narrowly self-interested sacrifices are in one way more self*less* (even though they might be more self*ish*) than are broadly self-interested or altruistic sacrifices. Narrowly self-interested sacrifices are more selfless in that they are not conditional upon a debt being incurred by the intended beneficiary of one's sacrifice but are, rather, a "gift" to our future selves (or future person-stages) to which no emotional strings have been attached.

On the basis only of the distinctions just made between cognitive and affective dispositions, on the one hand, and self- and other-regarding affective dispositions, on the other, we can partially explain why it seems to many people that in some of the puzzling examples in the personal identity literature, a person could for narrowly self-interested reasons choose to cease to exist in order to bring someone else into existence. Although the chooser, in these examples, may think he is sacrificing for someone else (say, one of his fission descendants), it still feels to the chooser as if he is sacrificing for himself. Affectively, the chooser will anticipate having the experiences that will be had by the intended beneficiaries of his choices; and the making of these sacrifices will be free of that emotional calculation that generates normative expectations of gratitude – free, that is, of "the you owe me" feeling. This account, simple as it is, can be used to resolve what may seem to be a deep puzzle about what matters in survival, which I shall call the "problem of exiting the loop." I shall return to this puzzle.

Consider, next, cognitive contextualizing, that is, the process of incorporating our salient experiences into narratives that in normal circumstances are our personal life histories. Most people, like Whiggish histo-

117

rians, regularly revise their personal narratives so that the past unfolds neatly into the present. Peter Berger gives several nice examples of this, some of which involve conversion experiences. In one of Berger's examples a person converts from being a conservative Christian to a hippie, after which he "realizes that the great emotional upheavals of the past were but puerile titillations" and that events of which he used to be proud, such as "the glowing day" when he was class valedictorian, have become embarrassing episodes in his "prehistory." These unwelcome memories are then pushed aside in the hippie's reconstructed biography to make room for events that he previously had regarded as unimportant, such as the time that he first tried to paint. Periodization also is affected profoundly. So, for instance, our newfound hippie, "instead of reckoning an era," as he had done before his conversion, from the date when he accepted Jesus at a church summer camp, may do so now "from that other date, previously one of anxious shame but now one of decisive self-legitimation" when he lost his virginity in the back seat of a car (Berger, 1963, p. 58).

Typically, episodes in our lives that we cognitively contextualize in this way are ones that have already happened. Sometimes, though, they are things that we think are about to happen. Hypothetical examples provide adequate evidence that many people, if they had real life identificatory surrogates, would regard events that have happened or that they believe are about to happen to their surrogates as they now regard events that have happened or that they believe are about to happen to themselves. For instance, if you had a fission descendant with whom you fully identified, then even though you did not believe that this person is you, you would regard events that happened to him or that you thought were about to happen to him just as you now regard events that have happened to you or that you believe are about to happen to you. However, you would not regard in the same way events that happened, or that you believed were about to happen, to someone who was neither yourself nor an identificatory surrogate for yourself.

Consider, next, that people act differently because of how they feel and think. In particular, there are distinctive behavioral consequences of the affective and cognitive ways in which people regard experiences they anticipate having. Perhaps any of these ways, individually, in which they act as a consequence of thinking and feeling things about the anticipated experiences of themselves or of their surrogate selves, is a way they might also act as a consequence of thinking and feeling related things about the anticipated experiences of others who are neither themselves nor their surrogate selves. But collectively these ways of acting tend to be distinctively linked to the anticipation of having either their own experiences or the experiences of their surrogate selves. As we shall see, it was in recognition of this that Priestley added to his observation that in his materialist version of the resurrection, "our personal identity will be sufficiently preserved," the rider, "and the expectation of it at present will have a proper influence on our conduct" (1777, pp. 166–7). He was reminding Christians not to worry that peoples' expecting the loss of their strict identities upon the occasion of their bodily deaths might defuse postresurrection scenarios of their power to keep us all in line; he claimed that whether or not our resurrected selves were strictly identical to our current selves, they would be *close enough* that our self-regarding affective anticipations of their experiences would be equally intimidating.

EXITING THE LOOP

It is noncontroversial that someone for altruistic reasons, say, to benefit his wife and children, might choose to cease to exist. It is relatively noncontroversial that someone for *broadly* self-interested reasons, say, to benefit himself indirectly by benefiting someone to whom his self-interest is already bound, such as his children, might choose to cease to exist. So, if any hypothetical examples, such as fission examples, in which people choose to cease to exist are to have startling implications for the importance of identity, the choices people make to cease to exist have to be *narrowly* self-interested. In addition, the choices have to seem to the people who make them to be their best choices even though they have other options that afford them a reasonable opportunity to persist in a normally desirable way.

What I am calling the "problem of exiting the loop" arises for examples that satisfy these conditions. The problem is that although it may seem *that* the chooser's motives in such examples could be narrowly self-interested, attempts to explain *how* they could be inevitably trace a thin line between sense and nonsense. It is as if one were trying to escape from a loop of interrelated concepts, with no way to do so. Consider, for instance, Parfit's attempts, in *Reasons and Persons,* to ask what is perhaps his central question regarding personal identity and what matters in survival:

> Personal identity is not what matters. It is merely true that, in most cases, personal identity coincides with what matters. What does matter *in the way in which* personal identity is mistakenly thought to matter? What is it rational to care about in our concern about our own future?
>
> The question can be restated. Assume, for simplicity, that it could be rational to be concerned only about one's own self-interest. Suppose that I

am an Egoist, and that I could be related in one of several ways to some resulting person. What is the relation that would justify egoistic concern about this resulting person? (1984, pp. 282–3)

Parfit intends these questions to include within their scope fission cases in which, he believes, identity is not preserved, but what matters in survival is obtained.

The problem of exiting the loop arises as soon as we ask what Parfit means by the expression, *in the way in which,* when he asks, "What does matter *in the way in which* personal identity is mistakenly thought to matter?" The expression cannot mean that personal identity matters in the way in which preserving ourselves *as the same persons* we now are matters; for if Parfit were asking us what matters in *that* way, in a situation in which we will not be preserved as the same persons, the answer, arguably, is "Nothing," and that is not the answer Parfit is trying to elicit. Similarly, Parfit's question, "What is it rational to care about in our concern about our own future," when asked of someone contemplating undergoing fission is tantamount to his asking, "What is it rational for you to care about in your concern about *your own future* in a situation in which *you* will not have a future?" Again, the answer may well be, "Nothing."

It does not help to restate the question in terms of egoism. On most theories of self-interest peoples' self-interest may be promoted not only by benefits that accrue to themselves alone but also by those that accrue to others – potentially *any* others; and their self-interest can be promoted even when they have to sacrifice to bring about such benefits to others. For instance, parents may promote their own self-interest by setting aside part of their income to be given to their children (or, for that matter, to anyone else) after they die. But if the members of one's bridge club, or even one's spouse or children, can be part of what it is rational for someone to care about in her self-interested concern for her *own* future, then apparently it can be rational for someone so motivated to care about *anyone.*

Other theorists have tried to sidestep this problem. Peter Unger, for instance, characterizes his central "prudential" sense of "what matters in survival" as what matters "from the perspective of a person's concern for herself, or *from a slight and rational extension of that perspective*" (Unger, 1991, p. 94). But Unger, then, never explains satisfactorily what the expression "slight and rational extension" means. And since virtually everything in his otherwise subtle and penetrating account of what matters in survival depends upon whether this "prudential" sense of "what matters in survival" is the correct notion to use to get at the questions he wants to ask, it is disturbing that, as in the case of Parfit's attempt to state his central question, it is unclear what he means.

The problem of understanding how such a chooser's motives could be narrowly self-interested might be solved easily if we were to suppose that those who choose to cease existing are sacrificing themselves to promote their most important egoistic projects – say, to ensure that someone will be around who is as disposed and able as they would be, were they alive and healthy, to finish writing their books. But in the situations depicted in these examples, many people, it seems, would choose to sacrifice their identities even if they had no project about which they cared all that much – none, that is, other than that of having a continuing opportunity to live a happy life. In addition, if we assume a three-dimensional view of persons, then in the fission examples many people, importantly because they feel – rightly or wrongly – that they can anticipate having the experiences of their fission descendants and performing their actions in pretty much the same ways that normally they anticipate having their own future experiences and performing their own future actions, would choose an option that would bring about their cessation. As we saw in Chapter 2, such motivations are quite different from interest in one's projects; and the anticipations that play a role in such motivations are quite different from the ways that typically one anticipates the experiences of closely related others, even others, such as one's children, to whom one is genetically and may be deeply emotionally linked and to whom one's self-interest may be closely bound.

It may seem that one might be able to dismiss the problem of exiting the loop on the grounds that if the puzzling choices are intended to be narrowly self-interested, then they are irrational. For instance, one might object that a choice to cease existing when one could choose continued worthwhile existence cannot possibly be rational because it would destroy the self whose interests one is supposedly trying to promote; or, one might object that one cannot rationally anticipate having another's experiences or performing her actions in pretty much the same ways one would anticipate having one's own future experiences or performing one's own future actions. But the former objection is not persuasive. A person may for narrowly self-interested reasons rationally sacrifice her existence to further her projects. And, as we saw in Chapter 2, apparently one cannot support the latter objection without begging the question.

Perhaps, then, one can dismiss the problem of exiting the loop by claiming that people who intentionally choose for narrowly self-interested reasons to cease in order to bring another person, or persons, into existence must be self-deceived. That is, in spite of what such people *say* they believe, what they must *really* believe is that their choices will preserve their identities. Suppose, though, that the choosers in the puzzling examples deny that they are the same people as any of the others for whom they sacrifice their existence and that they back up their denials in thoughtful and sophisticated ways (say, with Parfitian arguments). Unless they exhibit independent symptoms of having the alleged self-deceptive belief (an issue to which I shall return in the next chapter) it is question begging simply to insist that they *must* really believe that the so-called others for whom they sacrifice are themselves. The accusation of self-deception is especially dubious if there are alternative ways – as we shall see there are – of understanding self-interest and quasi-survival so as to make better sense of the puzzling examples.

Finally, it may seem that the problem under discussion arises only if we assume that people could not preserve their identities through fission of the sort described. Some – either because, like David Lewis, they subscribe to a four-dimensional view of persons or because, like John Perry, they question whether identity is transitive – may deny this assumption. But the problem arises also in connection with other examples, such as various teletransportation and transformation examples, none of which involve fission. Since I have argued for this in Chapter 4, I shall continue now, for expository purposes, to use fission examples as my illustrations, asking the reader to focus on what is crucial about them: not fission, but the apparently narrowly self-interested trading of continued identity for other benefits.

The difficulty, it seems, with our current understandings of self-interest, self-regard, egoism, and survival are that they lump all *others* into the same category. The puzzling examples suggest that there is something distinctive about certain others, or about the chooser's relation to them, that allows a choice to benefit these others to be more narrowly self-interested than a choice typically would be to benefit one's children, one's friends, or someone who could complete one's projects. But what? The simplest answer is that these others are the chooser's replicas. On this answer, the sacrifices people make to benefit either themselves or their replicas (or near-replicas) are narrowly self-interested, whereas the sacrifices they make to benefit anyone else, if they are not *also* sacrifices to benefit themselves or their replicas, are not narrowly self-interested. To see why this proposal will not work, one has only to remember Parfit's "branch-line" case, as it was elaborated earlier.

Perhaps, then, people are appropriate beneficiaries of narrowly self-interested choices not if they are replicas of the choosers but, rather, just if they are either the choosers themselves, the choosers' closest continuers, or someone who – as in the fission case – is tied with one or more others as the choosers' closest continuers (the branch-line replica fails to be such a continuer since he is upstaged by an even closer continuer). The relationship between choosers in the puzzling examples and such close-enough-continuers-than-which-none-is-closer is like the relationships between people and themselves in the future in that the choosers may believe that they can anticipate having the experiences of such continuers and anticipate performing their actions in pretty much the same ways they would anticipate having their own future experiences and performing their own future actions.

When used as a criterion of *identity*, the closest-continuer model includes a stipulation that continuers are close enough in the right respects to preserve identity (Nozick, 1981, p. 40). A similar stipulation would have to be included as part of the current proposal, except this time we would not insist that continuers are close enough in the right respects to preserve identity but only that they are close enough to preserve what matters most to their predecessors in their predecessors' concern for their own survival. For instance, continuers who, but for being tied with one or more others as closest continuers, would be close enough to preserve identity would be prime candidates to preserve what matters most to people in their concern for their survivals. But continuers might be much less close than that and still preserve what matters most. How much less close? And which characteristics of continuers are the salient dimensions along which closeness should be assessed? I shall suggest a way to begin to answer these questions.

First, though, I want to note that although these questions have never been answered satisfactorily in connection with the closest-continuer model of personal identity, they would have to be answered satisfactorily (and presumably also differently) to complete the proposal under consideration. Moreover, even if such a continuer proposal were correct in where it makes the cut between those who are appropriate beneficiaries of narrowly self-interested choices and those who are not, it would still not explain what makes it appropriate to make the cut at just that point. Without such an explanation we must rely upon intuitions about where the cut should be made. Notoriously, such intuitions tend to differ from person to person. Parfit, for instance, thinks that a teletransported replica is close enough in the right respects to be a beneficiary of narrowly self-interested choices; Unger thinks that people who consider the matter carefully may well not even want to endure a mild pain now so that their teletransported (closest-continuer) replicas could be spared much greater pain later.

In sum, there are three problems with resting content with a close-enough-continuer-than-which-none-is-closer model to solve the problem under discussion. The first – that of clarifying the criterion of closeness – is a problem with specifying the criterion clearly enough that it can be tested against our intuitions. The second – that of explaining why the cut should be made where even a clearly specified criterion says that it should be made – and the third – that of explaining differences of opinion about where the cut should be made – are problems with justifying and/or explaining our intuitions.

I have been focusing on objective ways in which a person can be related to others. My hope was to find a way of discriminating among others for the purpose of our anticipating having their experiences and performing their actions, that is, between those others who are and those others who are not appropriate surrogates for ourselves. It now seems that even were we to succeed in finding such an objective way of making this discrimination, we would still need a deeper explanation. Since objective sources of such an explanation have already been found wanting, the needed explanation, it would seem, can be found, if at all, only in our subjective relationships to others. Where, though, in our subjective relationships, can we find what we need to explain the intuitions that underlie principled ways of making the discrimination between those others who are and those others who are not appropriate surrogates for ourselves? The psychological process of identification, I think, is the most plausible place to seek for an answer to this question.

We tend to be willing to say that a choice to cease existing in order that someone else might begin to exist is narrowly self-interested to the extent that we, the choosers, identify with the intended, direct beneficiaries of our choices in the sense that we regard these beneficiaries who we do not believe are ourselves as if we did believe they were ourselves; in other words, the choice to cease existing seems to be narrowly self-interested to whatever extent we regard the intended direct beneficiaries of our choices as experiential and behavioral surrogates, in the relevant sense, for ourselves. In the case of teletransportation, for instance, those who put much more value on psychological continuity, however caused, than on bodily continuity have an easier time than do those who put a higher value on bodily continuity in identifying with their teletransported replicas and, hence, in regarding those replicas as appropriate beneficiaries of their narrowly self-interested choices to cease existing. And in the branch-line case, the reason it seems so obvious to almost everyone that the injured Earthling's sacrifice to benefit his Martian replica would not be narrowly self-interested is that few of us can empathize with the Earthling's identifying in such an intimate way with his Martian replica. In general, then, it would seem that whatever objective relationship choosers may have to the intended beneficiaries of their choices, if *the choosers* cannot identify, in the relevant sense, with these beneficiaries, then their choices to sacrifice for them will not seem *to the choosers* to be narrowly self-interested. And if *we* cannot empathize with their identifying with these intended beneficiaries, their choices will not seem *to us* to be narrowly self-interested. But how shall we understand *identification?* What is the *relevant* sense? We are now in a position to answer these questions.

Peoples' choices to cease existing to benefit continuers who they do not regard as themselves will seem narrowly self-interested to these people provided their self-regarding affective dispositions take these continuers as their objects. Their choices will seem narrowly self-interested to us provided that were we to put ourselves imaginatively into their places, our self-regarding affective dispositions would take these same continuers as their objects. Thus, for instance, for Parfit to ask the question he was trying to ask, he should not have asked, "What does matter *in the way in which* personal identity is mistakenly thought to matter?" but, rather, "What matters from the point of view of promoting the welfare of those future people who are objects of our self-regarding affective dispositions, regardless of whether we think those people are ourselves?" And instead of asking, "What is it rational to care about in our concern about our own future?" he should have asked, "What is it rational to care about in our concern about the future of those who are objects of our self-regarding affective dispositions?"

APPROPRIATION REVISITED

Returning now to the task of explaining surrogate-self-identification, I want to consider those cases, albeit rare, in which at least part of the appropriation involved in surrogate-self-identification is explicit. If, for the moment, we expand the scope of our concerns to include in addition to anticipation also memory, then ordinary forgetfulness provides a humdrum, but plentiful source of examples. For instance, I may take your word for it that I experienced being repaid the money you owed me even though I do not remember having had that experience. In such a case, a separate act of appropriation may be required for me to claim ownership of that experience. Because I do not remember the experience, it is not well integrated into the complex of affect, cognitive contextualizing, and behavioral change that does the appropriating work for me in other more central cases. But because you say I had the experience, even though I do not remember having had it, I believe you. I may even say, "I believe you." Such a separate act of appropriating, when it is explicit, is in cases like this usually, if not always, an attempt to facilitate the integration of the experience, or at least of one's claim now to have had it, into the relevant complex of affect, cognitive contextualizing, and behavioral change.

On the other hand, even though I do not consciously remember an experience, it may already be influencing my emotions and behavior, say, in case the experience was so painful that I have blocked it out of consciousness. But even in such cases, by declaring ownership of the experience I "officially" let it into the set of experiences that, among other things, I cognitively contextualize. Instances of this are common in psychotherapy. Recognition of the experience can "legitimize" it, thereby facilitating its integration into my life, perhaps even enhancing its influence (though not necessarily the same influence it had before) on my emotions and behavior.

More dramatic examples of explicit appropriation, and even of disappropriation, occur in the context of multiple personality disorder (or, as it is now called, "extreme dissociative disorder"), where the ownership of an action or of an experience may be contested by a multiple's different personas. Nellie Bean, for instance, was a patient of Morton Prince. In various of her personas, but particularly in one known as "B," she wrote autobiographies and also theorized about the origins of Nellie's dissociated personality. In B's writings, the issue of appropriation is never far from view, as the following quotations show: "Is she the only woman who ever kissed any man except her husband and is kissing a crime? And *she didn't do it anyway – I did it – myself* and it never hurt me a bit – I am glad of it – and she didn't have a husband anyway"; "I really came as a self at Nashua. *I ruled A* [another persona] *for weeks before I came* – she can't understand about that time, she was so well and strong and happy – but *it was I* . . . [T]hese thoughts and impulses and acts were *mine* not hers"; "You see *I know all that A thinks but I do not feel her emotions*"; "It is awfully mixed up – the shock that brought me as a personality woke that feeling [sexual desire] in A, and so she [A] thinks *that feeling belongs to me, but it doesn't,* I don't know anything about it except what she thinks" (Barresi, 1994, pp. 97, 101; emphasis added).

126

We have only to read such remarks to realize that the same sorts of explicit acts of appropriation and disappropriation that are a staple of B's commentary also occur in the lives of normal people. For instance, when people want to emphasize that an unwelcome feeling, thought, or action was not "in character" they might say some such thing as: "I was not myself last night," or even "The devil made me do it." When the feeling, thought, or action is welcome, then, whether or not it was "in character," they might say: "I've never felt more myself, never more real," and so on.

Sometimes, as the remarks of Rousseau quoted earlier remind us, we can relate to some real or fictional person's imagined experiences as if that person were either ourselves or one of our surrogate selves. But if we are psychologically healthy, our so identifying is quite transitory. It occurs, say, while we are totally absorbed in a book or a movie and wanes as soon as we get distracted. However, while we are actually in the throes of an identificatory fantasy, and to the extent that we are under its spell, then so far as our occurrent psychology is concerned, to a remarkable degree we may have overcome the boundaries between self and (fictionalized) other. Thus, without ever leaving the safety of our armchairs we can anticipate having, and actually have, fantasized surrogates of dangerous, exciting, and interesting experiences. Our ability to do this – to safely and conveniently acquire surrogate (partial) lives – is one of the main things that makes art, but particularly literature, theater, and film, so moving. But unless we are, or go, insane, the experience does not last long. Sooner or later (generally, sooner) the spell breaks and we are back into our own real and often drabber lives.

In sum, the proposal I have been developing is that ordinarily when a person surrogately self-identifies with a continuer, she does so just to the extent that certain of her psychological dispositions that normally would be directed only toward herself in the future are directed toward that continuer. I have given a sketchy account of what some of these dispositions are. Generally the appropriation in surrogate-self-identification is implicit in the functioning of these dispositions. As we have seen, in unusual cases it may also be explicit. For the purposes of what matters in survival (rather than for those of identity), this account also helps to explain how close a continuer has to be to qualify as a *close-enough-*continuer-than-which-none-is-closer; it also helps to explain which dimensions are the salient ones along which closeness should be measured.

Roughly speaking, for the purposes of what matters in survival a dimension is salient just if, and to the degree that, it facilitates surrogate-self-identification. Which dimensions these are vary from person to person and with the same person over time. However, in the case of one person at any given time, they collectively determine that a continuer is close enough to be a *close-enough*-continuer-than-which-none-is-closer so long as in at least one possible situation one can appeal to these dimensions to explain why it makes sense for that person – without altering her basic beliefs and values – to choose to cease to exist in order that a continuer who she does not believe is herself may begin to exist, even though she has other options that at least offer her a reasonable chance of persisting in a desirable way. Thus, such an account of identification helps to *explain* our intuitions – including how they differ from person to person – about where we should draw the line in determining which others are appropriate beneficiaries of narrowly self-interested choices.

In addition to explaining why people might regard continuers who they *do not* believe are themselves as appropriate beneficiaries of their *narrowly self-interested* choices, the account I have proposed is also revealing in the case of people who regard continuers they *do* believe are themselves as appropriate beneficiaries *only* of *broadly self-interested* or of *altruistic* choices. In the case, say, of people suffering from multiple personality disorder, one alter (i.e., the multiple in one of her personas) may well *feel* that sacrificing to benefit another alter is altruistic; and many of the multiple's interpretive cognitive dispositions may discriminate between herself in the role of one alter and another alter as if this other alter were another person. Indeed, not too long ago many therapists of such patients perceived the therapeutic task as that of convincing each alter to *sacrifice* her existence in favor of integrating with the others (Beahrs, 1982).

Yet if a multiple were philosophically sophisticated, she might believe theoretically, as many philosophers do, that in spite of how it feels to her subjectively, she is only one person regardless of which alter is in executive control. In other words, the multiple's theoretical cognitive dispositions might be out of sync with many of her other dispositions, but in the opposite way from the skeptic-about-self examples considered earlier. That is, theoretically the multiple in one of her personas may accept that she and the other alters are personas of the same person, even though many of the multiple's cognitive and affective dispositions function as if she and the alters were different persons. As a result, the multiple's choice to sacrifice in order to benefit someone *who she believes to be herself* might well feel like an altruistic or at least *broadly* self-interested choice, rather than like a *narrowly* self-interested one. The fact that the account of surrogate-self-identification developed in this chapter helps to explain this unusual feeling is evidence that it is true.

128

Still, it would seem that if the account I have sketched is true, there must be some underlying condition that explains why the affective, cognitive, and behavioral dispositions I have discussed will in unusual (and often only hypothetical) circumstances take others as their objects. The possibility that I want now to explore is that there is something about the way we normally regard ourselves that accounts both for why our self-regarding dispositions normally take only ourselves as their objects and why, by its being projected onto another, they also will take these others as their objects. That is the project of the next chapter.

6

Experience

Most adults during most of their waking hours experience what they take to be themselves *as perceivers*. By "most adults" I mean most in modern industrialized cultures; people in so-called primitive cultures may be different. By "most adults experience what they take to be themselves as perceivers" I mean, roughly, that when most adults experience either their own internal states or objects in the world, they simultaneously experience what they (mistakenly) take to be themselves as fixed, continuous points of observation on those internal states or external objects. By "fixed" I do not mean fixed forever or fixed absolutely, but rather relatively stable as compared with the dynamism of most of the rest of experience.

I call this illusory experience of self the *perceiver-self phenomenon*. It is, I think, a profound form of alienation and, hence, of human suffering. And I think it figures importantly in the formation of core human values and in fear of death. However, in this chapter I want only to defend the much more modest claim that the influence of this phenomenon needs to be taken into account to understand surrogate-self-identification, in particular, why people tend to surrogately self-identify with certain real and hypothetical continuers and not with others.

First, I want to answer those philosophers – nurtured on Book I of Hume's *Treatise* – who are skeptical that they ever, let alone almost always, experience what they take to be themselves as perceivers. Richard Taylor, for instance, expresses what may be a common attitude. He says that we can know that there is no such experience of self because we can always say informatively what experiences are like, including illusory experiences, but we can never say informatively what the experience of self is like:

> One imagines that he is deeply, perpetually, unavoidably aware of something he calls "I" or "me" . . . [But] as soon as one begins to try saying *anything whatever* about this inner self, this central reality, he finds he can say *nothing at all*. It seems to elude all description. All one can do, apparently, is refer to it;

one can never say what is referred to, except by multiplying synonyms – as if the piling of names upon names would somehow guarantee the reality of the thing named! But as soon as even *the least description* is attempted, one finds that what is described is *indistinguishable from absolute nothingness*. (Taylor, 1963, p. 124; emphasis added)

What, then, on Taylor's view, should we say of those people who think, as many do, that they experience a self? Presumably, we should say that they are merely imagining that they have such an experience. But how could they be mistaken? Presumably, by reading too much into the experiences they actually have; that is, by confusing an interpretation (or theory) of their experiences with the experiences themselves. In other words, they are misled by theories or presuppositions, perhaps derived from common sense, that they bring to their experiences, into thinking that they experience something they do not actually experience.

A problem with this idea is that one's theories or presuppositions can influence the content of one's experiences (and not just what one thinks is the content of one's experiences). Consider, for instance, the sensory illusions depicted in Figure 3. Each of these results not from a defective stimulus, say, from a distorted image on the back of the retina, but, rather, from the brain's subsequent conceptualization or interpretation (on "theoretical" grounds?) of an undistorted stimulus. That is, each depends on an interpretation – actually, a misinterpretation – of a sensory stimulus. Yet the result is an experience, albeit an illusory experience. Indeed, the result is an experience that is remarkably stable and robust. When one tries to describe such experiences one does not find that what one tries to describe is "indistinguishable from absolute nothingness." If that were true, the three illusory experiences just illustrated would be indistinguishable from each other. Obviously they are not.

By the same token, then, if there were an interpretation-induced or theory-induced (illusory) experience of a perceiver-self phenomenon it would still be an experience and presumably one with a describable phenomenology. And it too might be remarkably stable and robust. I claim that there is such an experience, that it is describable, and also that it is remarkably stable and robust. However, Taylor is right that it is hard to describe without "multiplying synonyms" and, hence, that it is hard to describe informatively.

An important part of the reason the perceiver-self phenomenon is hard to describe is that it is not like the veridical experience of any external object, for instance, the experience of seeing one line as longer than

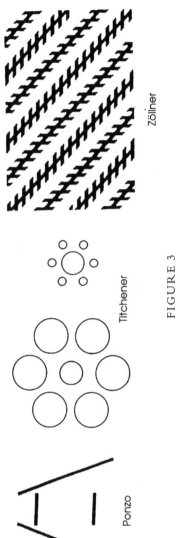

Ponzo

Titchener

Zöllner

FIGURE 3

another or one circle as bigger than another. This observation, while it might answer Taylor's objection, still is unlikely to persuade many skeptics. For it does not speak to what is surely the crucial source of skeptical doubt, namely, that many people, and perhaps most analytic philosophers, believe they cannot discover in their own experience any such perceiver-self phenomenon. How is it possible that such a pervasive experiential phenomenon could be so often overlooked, even by thoughtful, sophisticated people who are carefully trying to find it?

The main obstacle to finding it, I think, is confusion about what one is looking for. We need to overcome this obstacle to go further. I want, then, to begin by pointing out a vivid and stable instance of a perceiver-self phenomenon in an extraordinary experience, though one that is readily available. I call this experience, the "many-selves experience." By pointing out the perceiver-self phenomenon in it, I hope to clarify the perceiver-self phenomenon that I claim is also a feature of ordinary experience. That is the first step. Then I shall explain why we have to acknowledge the presence of a perceiver-self phenomenon in ordinary experience in order to account for a contrast between ordinary experience and what I shall call the "no-self experience." This explanation will also reveal why the perceiver-self phenomenon is such an elusive feature of ordinary experience and thereby, I hope, render it less elusive. That is the second step. Finally, I want to explain the relevance of the perceiver-self phenomenon to the debate over egoistic survival values.

THE MANY-SELVES EXPERIENCE

What I am calling the "many-selves experience" is an introspective dissociation between two "selves": a private "watcher-self" and the public self one shows to the world. This dissociation is the subjective side of the objective commonplace that each of us every day plays behavioral roles. These roles vary with our circumstances. We may, so to speak, be one person at the office, another at home with the spouse and kiddies, still another bowling with the buddies, and so on, these different sides of ourselves displayed in differences in interest, mood, desire, and energy level. For present purposes what is crucial about our role playing is that when we are experientially aware *while* we are playing a role *that* we are playing it, our individual subjective experiences may coalesce around two "selves," one of which, but only one of which, seems to be aware of the other. Consider, for instance, the following extraordinary (for reasons I shall explain) poem:

I know you, you shamster. / I saw you smirking, grinning, / Nodding through the day. / And I knew you lied. / With mincing steps you gaited before men, / Shouting of your valor. / Yet you, you idiot, / I knew you were lying. / And your hands shook. / And your knees were shaking. / I know you, you shamster. / . . . You are the me the world knows. (Braude, 1990, pp. 161–2)

Patience, the author of this poem, adopted a private perspective for observing and commenting on the version of herself that she showed to the world. If she adopted this perspective while she was performing the actions of her own that she is here criticizing, probably she had a many-selves experience. (But that is not why the poem is extraordinary.)

Another example of the same phenomenon would be someone who as therapy for routinely getting embarrassed in certain kinds of social situations is told to "watch" himself getting embarrassed without the "part" that is watching commenting on or judging, or trying to control, the embarrassment; that is, he is told that the part that is watching is *just* to watch. People who have never tried this are generally surprised to discover that the "part" of themselves that they have dissociated seems not only to be watching but also watching without embarrassment the rest of themselves get embarrassed. In other words, a person doing this will seem to have a "watcher-self" that does not experience *his* embarrassment as *its* embarrassment. More extreme examples of this phenomenon occur in some out-of-body experiences and in some dissociative reactions to intense pain.

Practiced habitually, the sort of dissociation just illustrated can lead to a dual inner life. Jorge Borges describes such a life – his own – in his charming and phenomenologically precise, "Borges and I":

> The other one, the one called Borges, is the one things happen to . . . I know of [him] from the mail and see his name on a list of professors or in a biographical dictionary. I like hourglasses, maps, eighteenth-century typography, the taste of coffee and the prose of Stevenson; he shares these preferences, but in a vain way that turns them into the attributes of an actor . . . I live, let myself go on living, so that Borges may contrive his literature, [but] . . . I am destined to perish . . . Little by little, I am giving over everything to him, though I am quite aware of his perverse custom of falsifying and magnifying things. (Borges, 1962, pp. 240–2)

An analogous sort of dissociation can take an intellectual turn, as in Thomas Nagel's account of "the true [objective] self":

Essentially I have no particular point of view at all, but apprehend the world as centerless. As it happens, I ordinarily view the world from a certain vantage point, using the eyes, the person, the daily life of TN as a kind of window. But the experiences and the perspective of TN with which I am directly presented are not the point of view of the true self, for the true self has no point of view and includes in its conception of the centerless world TN and his perspective among the contents of that world. It is this aspect of the self which is in question when I look at the world as a whole and ask, "How can TN be me? How can I be TN?" And it is what gives the self-locating philosophical thought its peculiar content. (Nagel, 1986, p. 61)

In each of the cases of Patience, Borges, and Nagel, there is simultaneously one person and two self-phemomena. However, whereas Nagel may not be talking about an experience but, rather, about a thought or conception, Patience probably and Borges almost surely are describing their own experiences. And whereas Nagel describes "the true self" as surveying the whole world as well as the particular person TN, Patience and Borges describe watcher-selves that, so far as their accounts go, merely survey their public selves. These differences aside, Nagel's conception of the true self embodies a conceptual dissociation that raises problems of identity similar to those raised by the experiential dissociations of Patience and Borges. That is, from the perspective of "the true self," Nagel wonders how "*he*" could be TN, whereas Patience and Borges, from their dissociated perspectives, simply presuppose that, whoever "*they*" are, they are not P and LB.

I am interested primarily in the two experiential dissociations. Phenomenologically, they share three features: first, the partitioning of subjective psychological space into a watcher-self and a public-self; second, the assignment of at least some experiences to one of these selves rather than to the other (e.g., when one watches "oneself" get embarrassed and simultaneously realizes that the "watching" part does not itself feel embarrassed, perhaps even feels some normally incompatible emotion, such as humor at the public self's embarrassment, generally the watching and the feeling of humor will be experienced as belonging to one self, or at least to one part of the psyche, and the embarrassment to another); and, third, the experiential illusion that the watcher-self is aware of the public self, including the public self's subjective states, such as its embarrassment, but not vice versa (i.e., it seems experientially that the watcher-self is a watcher, or a perceiver, in a way in which the public self that the watcher-self seems to be watching is not).

135

In characterizing this third feature of the dissociations, I say, "seems to be a perceiver," not "is a perceiver." I assume that, strictly speaking, neither dissociated self is a perceiver. Rather, both so-called selves are alike in being merely part of the content of experience or awareness. It is the person (or his brain), not either of the selves that are part of the person's (or, the brain's) experience, that is aware. This fact – in effect, Hume's lesson for those (unlike Hume in Book I) who accept the existence of material brains in addition to subjective experiences (Hume's "perceptions") – partly explains why the experience of a perceiver-self phenomenon is an illusion. That is, the experience is illusory partly because something that is not an experiencer is represented in experience as if it were. It is also illusory because something that is not fixed and continuous is represented in experience as if it were (but, for present purposes, and to keep our discussion as simple as possible, we can afford to ignore these two aspects of the illusion).

Illusory or not, the watcher-self seems to be a perceiver; that is, it is experienced as if it were a perceiver, and it continues to seem to be a perceiver if one examines it more closely. For present purposes, this is a huge advantage. For in the many-selves experience the experience of the perceiver-self phenomenon stands still long enough for us to get a good look at it. This is one of the things that was needed to make the case that there is such a phenomenon. To detect the perceiver-self phenomenon even in ordinary experience we need now to sharpen our understanding of it by comparing the many-selves experience (and the dissociation in it) with two closely related sorts of experiential dissociations with which the many-selves experience is easily confused. I shall call these the "alter-self experience" and the "experience of self-definition."

THE ALTER-SELF EXPERIENCE

The easiest access to the alter-self experience is through accounts of the phenomenology of automatic writing. William James has related such an account, by Sidney Dean, a journalist and member of the U.S. Congress from 1855 to 1859. Dean wrote:

> The writing is in my own hand but the dictation [is] not of my own mind and will . . . and I, myself, consciously criticize the thought, fact, mode of expressing it, etc., while the hand is recording the subject matter and even the words impressed to be written . . . Sentences are commenced without knowledge of mine . . . It is an intelligent *ego* which writes, or else the influence assumes individuality, which practically makes of the influences a

personality. It is *not* myself; of that I am conscious at every step. (James, 1890, I, p. 395)

The subjective experience of what Dean says is an "intelligent *ego* which writes," which he experienced as an other (i.e., not himself), is what I want to call the "alter-self phenomenon." It is whatever phenomenologically represents the experiential feeling that automatic writers typically have that some agent is internally influencing their bodily movements without being under their conscious control.

Since alter-selves (to speak of them, for the moment, as if they were agents) often express themselves in writing just as a person would, their influence is usually experienced by their host, that is, by the person in whom they reside, as if these alter-selves had a subjective psychology – beliefs, desires, intentions, and so on. They are experienced that way even though their host does not have introspective access to the alter-self's subjective psychology. This is a key difference between the many-selves experience and the alter-self experience. It is a difference that is related to how identification typically enters into these two sorts of experiences. In Dean's case, for instance, it seemed to him as if an *alien* self internally controlled his hand to express ideas that he did not consciously think or even necessarily consciously endorse. That is, it seemed to him as if his body, or part of it, were somehow "possessed," a typical feature of the alter-self experience and one that may explain why spiritualists often warn against the use of instruments for automatic writing (e.g., Ouija boards) on the grounds that they give alien and sometimes malevolent spirits a way of exerting influence in the human world.

Typically in automatic writing the action of such "spirits" is benevolent or neutral. It was in the case of Mrs. Curran, a St. Louis housewife and perhaps the most accomplished (certainly the most celebrated) automatic writer ever. When Mrs. Curran began playing on the Ouija board she had not graduated from high school. She had shown no evidence of literary ability or interest. But, then, Patience Worth introduced herself to Mrs. Curran on the board and took over guidance of Mrs. Curran's hand. Soon Mrs. Curran abandoned the Ouija board and Patience dictated to her directly. With Patience's help, Mrs. Curran then became a successful author. Between 1917 and 1928 she published five novels (under the name of Patience Worth). The novels had some literary merit and were favorably reviewed at the time (Hilgard, 1977, p. 136).

In Mrs. Curran's alter-self experience it seemed to her as if Patience Worth had an inner subjective psychology to which Mrs. Curran had no more conscious access than she had to the inner lives of other people. This phenomenon of limited access may have been iterated. Patience – not Mrs. Curran – implies, in her poem quoted earlier, that she too – Patience – has dissociated into a watcher-self and a public self. *That* is why the poem is so extraordinary.

THE EXPERIENCE OF SELF-DEFINITION

The many-selves experience might also be confused with the experience of *self-definition,* that is, with an experience in which someone sheds a familiar self-conception and adopts a new one. An example that will be familiar to many is Sartre's well-known characterization of the Peeping Tom. Totally absorbed in the scene he is observing, this person is suddenly discovered and then "objectified," by being labeled, "peeper." He is labeled, first, by the person who catches him and, then, by himself (Sartre, 1966, pp. 348–51). If his accepting the label "peeper" were dramatically to upset how he normally represents himself to himself in his experience (the representation is via his self-image), then in suddenly switching to his new way of representing himself he would be having an experience of self-definition, as I am understanding that phenomenon. That is, in what I am calling "experiences of self-definition," people cast off familiar, perhaps "private," self-conceptions and adopt unfamiliar, perhaps "public" ones. Other examples include certain deeply moving experiences in which people admit to themselves for the first time that they are alcoholics or homosexuals.

A different sort of example of this same phenomenon occurs in Toni Morrison's novel *Sula.* The passage is about a young adolescent:

> Late that night after the fire was made, the cold supper eaten, the surface dust removed, Nel lay in bed thinking of her trip . . . It had been an exhilarating trip but a fearful one . . . But she had gone on a real trip, and now she was different. She got out of bed and lit the lamp to look in the mirror. There was her face, plain brown eyes, three braids and the nose her mother hated. She looked for a long time and suddenly a shiver ran through her.
> "I'm me," she whispered. "Me."
> Nel didn't know quite what she meant, but on the other hand she knew exactly what she meant.
> "I'm me. I'm not their daughter. I'm not Nel. I'm me. Me."
> Each time she said the word *me* there was a gathering in her like power, like joy, like fear. Back in bed with her discovery, she stared out the window at the dark leaves of the horse chestnut.

"Me," she murmured. And then, sinking deeper into the quilts, "I want . . . I want to be . . . wonderful. Oh, Jesus, make me wonderful." (Morrison, 1973, pp. 28–9)

As this example vividly illustrates, at the core of an experience of self-definition is a judgment on the part of the person who has it that "I am this and not that." Typically, such judgments are made by people in the throes of a sudden shift of identifications that leaves them with unfamiliar loci of identity with which they then have to deal. Thus, experiences of self-definition tend to be poignant; for instance, they may be profoundly liberating (Nel's), or acutely uncomfortable (the peeper's), or attended by a tremendous release of tension (the alcoholic's or the homosexual's), or all of these at once.

One thing that all experiences of self-definition have in common is that they seem to reveal to the people who have them deep personal truths about themselves. That is why these experiences are a ready vehicle for personal transformation, and also why they deserve more attention philosophically – from moral psychologists – than they have received (so far as I know, they've received almost none). For present purposes the important point is that *if* the experience of a perceiver-self phenomenon were *simply* one form of the experience of self-definition, *then* putative experiences of a perceiver-self phenomenon might be explained simply as shifts in identification. And since experiences of self-definition of the sort illustrated are relatively rare – most people do not often have an occurrent concern about who they are – there may not be much reason to think that acts of identification are deeply implicated in most peoples' ordinary moment-to-moment experience.

There is more to the experience of the perceiver-self phenomenon than simply the acts of identification that are central to experiences of self-definition. People *could* have experiences of self-definition in which they experience themselves not as *perceivers* but as bundles of Humean *perceptions*. And if someone did have such an experience, he would not in it experience himself as a perceiver-self at all. Carl Jung, toward the end of his life, may actually have had such an experience, which he reported as follows:

> I had the feeling that everything . . . I aimed at or wished for or thought, the whole phantasmagoria of earthly existence, fell away or was stripped from me – an extremely painful process. Nevertheless something remained; it was as if I now carried along with me everything I had ever experienced or done, everything that had happened around me. I might also say: it was with

139

me, and I was it. I consisted of all that, so to speak. I consisted of my own history, and I felt with great certainty: this is what I am. "I am this bundle of what has been, and what has been accomplished." (Jung, 1961, p. 290)

Jung's experience soon transformed from the phase here described into one that was more complicated and ambiguous. But in this initial phase it was an experience that if not all that a Humean might hope for, is at least close. In particular, Jung's experience, in its initial phase, was both one of self-definition and one that seems not to have included a perceiver-self phenomenon. That is one part of what's important about Jung's experience. The other part is that in its being both an experience of self-definition and one that seems not to have included a perceiver-self phenomenon, his experience was very unusual. That strongly suggests that more normal experiences of self-definition do include perceiver-self phenomena, in which case experiences of perceiver-self phenomena cannot simply be understood in terms of shifting patterns of identification of the sort that occur in experiences of self-definition (such as Jung's).

In fact, such identifications as do occur in experiences of self-definition have more to do, it would seem, with who (or what) one feels one really is than with the different intimation, which is characteristic of the perceiver-self phenomenon, of one's somehow being a watcher or perceiver. What is needed, then, to clarify the perceiver-self phenomenon is a way to bring this extra, mysterious element of its content into clearer focus. To do that I want to contrast the many-selves experience, in which, as we've seen, there is not only a perceiver-self phenomenon, but one that stands still, with its polar opposite, the no-self experience, in which there is no perceiver-self phenomenon whatsoever.

THE NO-SELF EXPERIENCE

Esoteric no-self experiences are a staple feature of the literature of mysticism – particularly but not exclusively (consider Meister Eckhart) of Asian mysticism. In classical Theravada Buddhist texts, for instance, shedding what I have called the perceiver-self phenomenon is called, "dispelling the illusion of compactness" (Vajirañana, 1975; Nyanamoli, 1976). Jack Engler nicely describes the process:

> My sense of being an independent observer disappears. The normal sense that I am a fixed, continuous point of observation from which I regard now this object, now that, is dispelled. Like the tachistoscopic flicker-fusion phenomenon which produces the illusion of an "object" when discrete and

discontinuous images are flashed too quickly for normal perception to distinguish them, my sense of being a separate observer or experiencer behind my observation or experience is revealed to be the result of a perceptual illusion, of my not being normally able to perceive a more microscopic level of events. When my attention is sufficiently refined through training and kept bare of secondary reactions and elaboration of stimuli, all that is actually apparent to me from moment to moment is a mental or physical event and an awareness of that event. In each moment there is simply a process of knowing (nama) and its object (rupa). Each arises separately and simultaneously in each moment of awareness. No enduring or substantial entity or observer or experiencer or angesn – no self – can be found behind or apart from these moment-to-moment events to which they could be attributed (an-atta = no-self). In other words, the individual "frames" appear which had previously fused in normal perception in a tachistoscopic manner to produce an apparently solid and fixed image of a "self" or an "object." The only observable reality at this level is the flow of mental and physical events themselves. There is no awareness of an observer. There are just individual moments of observation. (Engler, 1986, pp. 41–2)

That is the most phenomenologically precise description, of which I'm aware, of experiencing in a state of heightened sensitivity without the perceiver-self phenomenon.

Jiddhu Krishnamurti has characterized somewhat more poetically what I think is a similar experience:

In ancient China before an artist began to paint anything – a tree, for instance – he would sit down in front of it for days, months, years, it didn't matter how long, until he *was* the tree . . . This means that there was no space between him and the tree, no space between the observer and the observed, no experiencer experiencing the beauty, the movement, the shadow, the depth of a leaf, the quality of colour. He was totally the tree, and in that state only could he paint. (1969, pp. 95–6)

Krishnamurti contrasts this unusual psychological state with the *seeming* (but not actual) divisiveness of most ordinary experience:

Now, when I build an image about you or about anything, I am able to watch that image, so there is the image and the observer of the image . . . [T]he observer is separate from the thing he observes. But . . . [the observer] is made up of memories, experiences, accidents, influences, traditions and infinite varieties of suffering, all of which are the past . . . [T]here is a central image put together by all the other images, and this central image, the observer, is the censor, the experiencer, the evaluator, the judge. (p. 96; see also the section on identification in Krishnamurti, 1997)

141

And Charlotte Joko Beck has made much the same point by remarking that while it certainly "looks" to each of us as though we are "separate from other people and from all else in the phenomenal world," which she says is a source of "much misery," what "we call the self is no more than a series of thoughts" to which "we're attached" (Beck, 1993, pp. 75, 78). In sum, what Krishnamurti has called, the "observer," and Beck has called, the "self," and what I am calling the "perceiver-self phenomenon" apparently is a construct out of what Hume called "perceptions." And it is brought into being by identification with the perceptions out of which it is constructed.

Such identification, I have argued, consists in dispositions to think, feel, and behave in various ways, some of which were sketched in Chapter 5. These dispositions structure our experiences so that it seems experientially (but not necessarily intellectually) *to* each of us as if the following were true *of* each of us: I am a perceiver who is somehow included in my experience as an observer of my experience. That part of our experiences – the perceiver-self phenomenon – that seems experientially as if it were us is experienced as if it were a perceiver, even though it is not. So, it is an experiential illusion. Yet, even though it is illusory, it still may be – in the views of Krishnamurti and Buddhists actually is – a stubborn feature of most peoples' ordinary experience. And it may be a feature of experience that persists, ordinarily, even in people, such as many Buddhist meditators, who understand intellectually and perhaps even through esoteric experiences that it is an illusion.

What I am calling "esoteric no-self experiences" are not "mystical" in the sense that they are ineffable. They are as effable as any similarly complex and unusual subjective experiential state. They are merely hard to describe. For present purposes, what is important is not describing them relatively fully and clearly, but merely pointing out that they contrast *dramatically* with ordinary (normal) experiences in that they do not include a perceiver-self phenomenon. And, luckily, this feature of them is rather easy to describe (indeed, I just did it). By contrast, as has been claimed, in the case of adults, most, but not all, ordinary experiences do include a perceiver-self phenomenon. It is this experiential contrast that is of interest.

The best way to understand esoteric no-self experiences is to have one. Unfortunately one cannot just make that happen. The next best way is to compare reports of esoteric no-self experiences with your own understanding of a kind of no-self experience that you have had that is not unusual. For instance, consider what your experience was like during periods of extreme concentration, such as when you were totally absorbed in working on an intellectual problem. Or consider what it was like at times when your activity was sensually overwhelming, say, during sex or swimming, or listening to music. Probably at some such times you were, as we say, totally "lost" in your activity. If you were, then there was no psychological distance – no sense of separation – between you and your focus of attention. That is, there was no self-consciousness (of a divisive sort) in your experience. I shall call such experiences "common no-self experiences." We have all had them. For present purposes, an interesting feature of common no-self experiences is that, almost always, they end as soon as one introspects. The reason they end is that, almost always, when one introspects, a perceiver-self phenomenon returns and with it the psychological distance.

It may seem that the important difference between ordinary experiences that include what I am calling the perceiver-self phenomenon and no-self experiences, whether esoteric or common, is just that in ordinary experiences you are aware of your body (or of internal bodily sensations) in addition to whatever may be the external focus of your attention, whereas in no-self experiences this awareness of your body (or of internal bodily sensations) falls away. This is not the important difference. For one thing, in sensually overwhelming *common* no-self experiences, such as may occur, for instance, during sex or swimming, your body may be the focus of your experience. For another, in *esoteric* no-self experiences one often has a heightened awareness of one's body and of internal bodily sensations (recall the quoted remarks by Engler). The crucial difference between ordinary experiences and no-self experiences is that in ordinary experiences, whether or not one is aware of one's body or of internal bodily sensations, one experiences oneself as a perceiver and in no-self experiences one does not.

In common no-self experiences the psychological distance "between observer and observed" that is such a persistent feature of ordinary experience disappears. What seems to collapse this sense of distance is that one's attention is totally absorbed by some object or activity. Break the absorption, say, by introspecting, and the sense of distance returns. In esoteric no-self experiences, on the other hand, concentration on or absorption in an object or activity generally is not necessary to keep the perceiver-self phenomenon at bay. At such times one may even carefully introspect in search of a perceiver-self phenomenon without its reappearing. That is, in esoteric no-self experiences it is not just that one introspectively looks for and then fails to find a perceiver-self phenomenon – any neo-Humean, at

143

almost any time, can do that on demand – but, rather, that the same sort of immediacy and lack of distance that is a feature of the common no-self experience is a feature even of one's relaxed introspective survey. For present purposes, that is the key difference between common no-self experiences and many esoteric no-self experiences described in the literature of mysticism.

ANALYSIS OF THE PERCEIVER-SELF PHENOMENON

I have suggested, first, that in most ordinary experiences one experiences a sense of psychic distance between oneself as perceiver and the objects of one's perception – an experience of separation between "the observer and the observed"; second, that this sense of psychic distance is not present in either sort of no-self experience; third, that in common no-self experiences the separation – the observer – tends to reappear as soon as one relaxes one's concentration, which happens, almost always, when one reflects on or introspects the experience; and, finally, that in esoteric no-self experiences there not only is no sense that an observer is present, but there may continue to be no sense that one is present even when one relaxes one's concentration and even when one is reflecting on or introspecting one's experience. How, then, should we understand the perceiver-self phenomenon?

For one thing, the perceiver-self phenomenon, which is a sensed separation between oneself as (hidden) perceiver and the objects of one's perception, is felt or experienced, rather than thought. Its presence or absence in one's experience is independent of theories or views one might hold – at least at the ordinary level at which we subscribe to theories and views – about what one can identify introspectively. When a perceiver-self phenomenon is present in someone's experience, that person is not "one with" his experience – that is, his experience is not characterized by the unifying immediacy of either esoteric or common no-self experiences – and this quite apart from what views he may have about the presence or absence of a perceiver-self phenomenon in his experience.

Failure to appreciate the independence of the perceiver-self phenomenon from one's theories about whether any such phenomenon is present frequently leads to philosophical misunderstanding. For instance, many analytic philosophers have no trouble agreeing with Buddhist meditators that the self is an illusion. Yet the philosophers totally misunderstand the experiential basis for the meditators' claim. This is shown by the fact that the philosophers often wonder why the meditators think that what the

144

philosophers regard as a philosophical commonplace – that the self is an illusion – is such a big deal. And, of course, in this day and age, *theoretically* this commonplace no longer is a big deal. But *experientially* it is. The difference between the philosopher who accepts theoretically that the self is an illusion and the meditator who has realized experientially that the self is an illusion is immense. Ironically, generally the philosopher will be basing his claim partly on his failure to discover introspectively a perceiver-self phenomenon in experiences in which it is nevertheless present, that is, in experiences in which there is a felt distance, which he has not noticed, between observer and observed. The meditator, if he is reporting on his experiences and not just repeating something he has heard or read, will be basing his claim on an esoteric no-self experience.

In the perceiver-self phenomenon the self that seems to be doing the perceiving includes a "hidden core." This is not solely because one experiences oneself as a *perceiver*. In the many-selves experience, the public-self may be experienced as if it were some sort of perceiver every part of which – its experience of the public environment, as well as its internal sensations, such as embarrassment – is accessible to introspective examination and, hence, not "hidden." That is, in the many-selves experience the public-self-as-perceiver is accessible to introspection "objectively," that is, as if from a so-called third-person point of view. What I am calling the "perceiver-self phenomenon," by contrast, is the experiential sense both that there is a (hidden) subject – a perceiver – of one's experience that is not itself among the objects of one's experience and that this subject is oneself.

It is that latter aspect of a perceiver-self phenomenon, the experience of the (illusory) subject of experience as oneself, that makes the perceiver-self phenomenon relevant to the topic of surrogate-self-identification. For what, one might ask, does the person whose "self" is implicated in the perceiver-self phenomenon in her own experience, suppose, perhaps unconsciously, is going to become of this self when she undergoes some exotic transformation, such as fission or teletransportation? Surely, with regard to the examples discussed in the personal identity literature, how that question is answered could help to explain why people identify or fail to identity with hypothetical continuers of themselves. That is why the perceiver-self phenomenon is relevant to the philosophical discussion of what matters in survival.

Returning to our analysis of the perceiver-self phenomenon, the aspect of this experience that I called the "hiddenness of the self" is especially apparent in a many-selves experience in which, say, one might introspect the watcher-self's experiences – for instance, its humor at the public self's embarrassment. But one cannot introspect the watcher-self-qua-perceiver without changing it into a kind of internal "public self" that is itself upstaged by another "higher-order" watcher-self that is itself hidden. That is, insofar as phenomenology is concerned, the "self" that is implicated in the perceiver-self phenomenon always perceives as if from "behind" experience. If one tries to experience this self as an object of perception, one of two things will happen: Either the "self" implicated in the original perceiver-self phenomenon is "upstaged" by a higher-level "self," or else one dissolves the perceiver-self phenomenon altogether (though not necessarily *all* experienced duality between self and other). The former is the overwhelmingly more likely outcome. It is what happens when one introspects for a perceiver-self phenomenon and fails to find one even though it is present in one's experience. The latter is what happens in an esoteric no-self experience.

The clearest way to get an experiential focus on the perceiver-self phenomenon would be to have an experience that does not include it, that is, to have a no-self experience, and then to notice, by carefully introspecting while one is having the experience, its dramatic contrast with ordinary experience. In common no-self experiences one does not introspect, and hence one does *not* notice by carefully introspecting *while* one is having the experience that no perceiver-self phenomenon is present. So, unless one has an esoteric no-self experience, one is not likely to notice the difference between, on the one hand, introspecting for a perceiver-self and failing to find it when the experiential sense that there is a perceiver-self is nevertheless present and, on the other, introspecting for a perceiver-self and failing to find it when there is no experiential sense that there is a perceiver-self present. For unless one has an esoteric no-self experience one has no *experiential contrast while introspecting* on the basis of which one could notice the difference between the presence of a perceiver-self phenomenon and its absence. In other words, except in the case of esoteric no-self experiences there is always a felt distance between oneself and the objects of one's *introspective* experience. So it is difficult to notice that felt distance even when one, in introspection, looks specifically for it. It is as if the perceiver-self phenomenon were a background hum that has always been present and, hence, easily goes unnoticed. It is only when the perceiver-self phenomenon and with it the felt distance goes away – when the hum is replaced by silence – that one can appreciate *experientially* what its presence was like in the first place. *That is why the experiential sense that there is a perceiver-self is so elusive.*

What, then, phenomenologically, does a perceiver-self phenomenon consist in? Here, analysis can go only so far. One can say that it involves a partitioning of psychological space, not among experiences, but between experiences and a postulated psychic point. This, presumably, is what accounts for the phenomenon of distancing, or lack of immediacy, in ordinary experiences that distinguishes them so sharply from no-self experiences. Moreover, there is the experiential sense that this postulated point is a perceiver of experiences rather than itself an experience; that is, this psychological partitioning is not merely a partitioning but, rather, one that has a directional element – an asymmetry. This directional element is due to a hidden experiential reference back to a perceiver-self that seems to observe experiences and also seems not itself to be observed by experiences. In other words, the perceiver-self phenomenon is experienced only as the feeling that there is a perceiver behind experience (and therefore separate from it), and it is this feeling that creates the directional distancing. Beyond this the perceiver-self phenomenon seems to be unanalyzable, at least at the level of phenomenology. One cannot, so far as I can tell, say much more about what it consists in without simply "multiplying synonyms." So, Taylor was partly right. However, where Taylor and other skeptics about the experience of a perceiver-self phenomenon err is in supposing that since we cannot say any more about the perceiver-self phenomenon, there is no such phenomenon. I have urged, on the contrary, that only by acknowledging it can one explain certain contrasts among our experiences.

In this chapter I have argued, in effect, that while we have beliefs at what I am calling the "level of theory," we also have beliefs or something like them (say, *quasi-beliefs*) at the "level of experience." What we believe at the level of theory includes most of what we would say, if asked, about what we believe. In addition to such "theoretical" beliefs we may also experience the world *as if* we had certain other beliefs. Our experiencing the world as if we had these other beliefs is what I mean by *quasi-believing* at the level of experience.

I have argued that most of us most of the time experience what we take to be ourselves as perceivers. If I am right about that, this experiential quasi-belief may have to be taken into account in understanding surrogate-self-identification. And it may not be the only experiential quasi-belief that has to be taken into account. Michael Ayers, for instance, has claimed that the experience of "*ourselves* as being a material object among others" is one that "essentially permeates our sensory experience of things in general" (1991, II, p. 285). Persson has elaborated by suggesting that each of us perceives his own body, and only his own body, differently than he experiences other material objects. More specifically, he has said that whereas what we see and feel in the case of other material objects are "surfaces without depth," we are "proprioceptively aware of our own bodies as *filling* three-dimensional regions of space"; that is, we are aware of them as solids. Persson has conjectured that it is because of this proprioceptive awareness that we can feel bodily sensations, such as pains and hunger, inside our bodies and even at specific locations within our bodies, say, between where one feels pressure on one's back and an itch near one's navel (1996, pp. 24–9).

But what is not clear in the case of such identification with one's body is whether one experiences one's body as an item in phenomenal space or as an item in the objective world. It would seem, the former. So, for instance, an amputee can still feel a pain in her toe even while she holds before her mind the knowledge that she no longer has a toe. For certain purposes one apparently achieves some sort of "match" between the relative locations of items in phenomenal space and the relative locations of things to which we take them to correspond in physical space. And perhaps that is what we do normally with experiences of our bodies. And since the match is so habitual and so close it may never occur to us that the phenomenal space in which we experience our bodies and the physical space in which we suppose them to be located are not identical. Only in unusual circumstances will it be apparent that a matching of the two is even taking place.

Oliver Sacks, for instance, reports that "all amputees, and all who work with them, know that a phantom limb is essential if an artificial limb is to be used." Sacks quotes Dr. Michael Kremer, who says he is "quite certain that no amputee with an artificial lower limb can walk on it satisfactorily until the body-image, in other words the phantom, is incorporated into it." And Sacks himself reports on a patient under his care who described how he had to "wake up" his phantom in the mornings by flexing his thigh-stump toward himself and then slapping it sharply – "like a baby's bottom" – several times. Sacks says that according to the patient "on the fifth or sixth slap the phantom suddenly shoots forth, rekindled, fulgurated, by the peripheral stimulus" and that "only then can he put on his prosthesis and walk" (1985, p. 67). In the case, then, of Persson's example it seems clear that if one feels a pain between where one feels pressure on one's back and an itch near one's navel, one's feeling the pain there is a projection onto physical space of what one located initially in phenomenal space. One's feeling it phenomenologically does not necessarily depend (except perhaps causally) on one's body's even existing; for instance, as in the phantom limb phenomenon one could still feel the pain in that bodily location if one were a brain in a vat.

I think Ayers and Persson are right that normally we do experience ourselves as beings with bodies. Do we experience ourselves as beings who necessarily have our current bodies? There is an analogous question about our experience of the perceiver-self phenomenon. For reasons that are hard to articulate it does seem somewhat clearer that in the case of the perceiver-self phenomenon most of our perceptions of things include not only the illusion of there being in experience a perceiver, or a subject of experience, that we experience as ourselves, but also the experience of this subject as if it were necessarily ourselves. So, for instance, while our experience might not mitigate against our being teletransported and thereby acquiring a new body, it would mitigate against the subject of experience that is the experiential perceiver in this new body not being our current subject of experience. While this comparative judgment is mainly supported just intuitively, there is some slight clinical evidence for it. Sacks, for instance, says that "it is only by courtesy of proprioception, so to speak, that we feel our bodies as proper to us, as our 'property,' as our own" (1985, p. 43).

In reporting on the case of a woman who had a massive failure of proprioception and claimed to feel "disembodied," Sacks notes that the woman refused to reappropriate her body even as she gradually, over a period of several weeks, replaced the normal, unconscious feedback of proprioception, which she had lost, with an equally unconscious feedback that she had newly acquired. The new feedback was via vision together possibly with "a compensatory enhancement of the vestibular body-model or body-image," both of which normally are "subsidiary to the proprioceptive body-model." Sacks notes that although the woman "had learned to operate" physically, her eventually doing so, at least according to her, did not cause her sense of being disembodied to go away. The woman, he says, reported that she continued "to feel, with the continuing loss of proprioception, that her body is dead, not-real, not-hers – she cannot appropriate it to herself." As she put it (Sacks says, "These are her own words"), "I feel my body is blind and deaf to itself . . . it has no sense of itself" (p. 51).

Sacks says that when he originally reported on this woman's condition, cases of this sort were rare, but that later – in the 1980s – they became commonplace. Most of the newly afflicted, he reports, were health faddists who had been taking enormous quantities of Vitamin B_6 (pyridoxine)

149

(1985, pp. 53–4). Thus, Ayers's claim that peoples' experience of themselves "as being a material object" among others "essentially permeates" their sensory experience, while vague, perhaps could be refined and tested in the light of empirical data of the sort that emerges from the study of pathology. In the case of Sacks's patient, at least, it seems that while she may have experienced herself as being a material object among others, she did not include all of what we would regard as her body (and what she previously had regarded as her body) in that experience of her*self.*

However this question about Ayers's claim is resolved, it seems clear that peoples' theoretical beliefs and their experiential beliefs are not always in sync; in particular, people sometimes experience the world as if they had certain beliefs that they would not admit verbally that they have (not because they are lying but because whatever controls their speech mechanisms is not aware that they have any such beliefs). Some familiar instances of self-deception may be like this. Among most philosophical skeptics of the perceiver-self phenomenon, so also is the conflict between their quasi-belief at the level of experience that some part of what is represented in their experience is themselves-as-perceivers and their belief at the theoretical level that no such phenomenon exists.

Whether verbally acknowledged or not, an experiential quasi-belief might explain dispositions that the organism verbally acknowledges having. In the case of the quasi-belief ingredient in the perceiver-self phenomenon, it is possible that what explains why a person would anticipate having the experiences of someone who he does not believe, at the level of theory, is himself, is that, at the level of experience, he does quasi-believe that this person is himself. That is, it is possible that at the level of experience, someone might project the self that he is currently experiencing onto a continuer of his that at the level of theory he does not believe is himself, and that his doing this is what explains why the three characteristically self-regarding dispositions discussed in the preceding chapter take this continuer as their object.

What I am suggesting is that the three identificatory dispositions discussed in the preceding chapter might take a continuer as their object, even though the person who has these dispositions might – at the level of theory – regard this continuer as an other, because at the level of experience, which for the operation of these dispositions might be the level that matters, the person whose dispositions these are experiences this continuer as himself. If that were true, it would explain something that is otherwise puzzling, namely, why normally self-regarding dispositions suddenly cross the boundary between self and other, taking an other as their object. The explanation would be that these self-regarding dispositions do this because it is only at the level of theory that these objects are others; at the level of experience they are regarded as the same people on whom these dispositions are normally focused. In short, at least an important part of the reason that these dispositions would cross the theoretical boundary between self and other is that they never really cross the experiential boundary between self and other, and the experiental boundary is the one that really matters.

Our ability to project ourselves at the level of experience – either by projecting our identification with ourselves as perceivers or with ourselves as bodies in the world – could also explain what our anticipation of having humdrum experiences consists in. In the preceding chapter, we considered the example of someone's anticipating having the experience tomorrow of brushing his teeth. I suggested that it is not plausible to suppose, with respect to such anticipated experiences, that one's anticipation of having them consists in one's vividly and spontaneously imagining, from the inside, what they will be like. By the same token, it is also not plausible to suppose that one's anticipation of these experiences consists in revisions in the ways we cognitively contextualize our lives or in the ways we behave. It is not even plausible that one's anticipation of having such experiences consists in their becoming the object of our self-regarding affective dispositions, for in anticipating having really humdrum experiences we may not experience any affect at all.

Something else, then, must account for what our anticipating having these experiences consists in. The experiential projection of the perceiver-self phenomenon, or of ourselves as bodies, could account for it. That is, it may be that in someone's anticipating having the experience of brushing his teeth, he imagines that the same subject of experience that will be involved in the teeth brushing is the one he currently experiences. Alternatively, it could be that he imagines that the same body that will be involved is the body he currently identifies as his. It may seem that the example of teletransportation would defeat this latter possibility. But even if teletransportation were routine, people might still imagine, at the level of experience, that the same body would be involved in the replica's future teeth brushing even though at the level of theory they regarded the body that would be involved as a different one from their current body. However, even if some such speculations were correct, an additional account would still be needed to explain why in response to the puzzle cases in the personal identity literature people identify differently *from each other* with real and hypothetical continuers of themselves.

To identify at all with any aspect of your current self is already to drive a wedge between yourself and people who may continue you in various respects but not closely enough, or not in the right respects, to be you (according to some criterion of personal identity to which you subscribe). Perhaps, then, part of the explanation of the differing responses that people have to the puzzle cases lies also in the fact that people differ in the degrees to which they experientially identity with any aspect of their current selves. In addition, even if one identifies with one's psychology, rather than one's body, there is still the question of whether, to identity with a future continuer, one must have one's numerically identical psychology or whether a qualitatively similar psychology would do as well. In general, it seems, the more that one identifies in some way with some aspect of one's current self and then extends that identification only to continuers who retain the very same numerically identical aspects, the more conservative one is likely to be in identifying with real or hypothetical continuers of oneself that one believes at the theoretical level are not oneself. In short, the more conservatively inclined have a greater tendency to hold on, the more liberally inclined to let go. However, the realization that one's identifying experientially either with one's psychology or one's body is almost always going to involve an illusion – for instance, either that one experiences oneself as an observer of one's other experiences, or that one experiences ones' bodily sensations as items in physical space, rather than simply as items in phenomenal space – tends, I think, to weaken one's disposition to so identify, and, hence, to make one more liberal.

In sum, in trying to account in the preceding chapter for what it means to anticipate having experiences that one imagines will be had by someone in the future, I argued that this anticipation may just consist in the fact that a variety of normally self-regarding dispositions take this person (or person-stage) in the future as their object. When this person in the future is oneself, nothing will seem amiss. However, when this person in the future is an other – as, say, a three-dimensionalist about persons would believe of her fission descendants – one encounters the odd phenomenon of these normally self-regarding dispositions now taking an other as their object. Why do they do that?

For three-dimensionalists about persons it is tempting to suppose that they do it because fundamentally they are not self-regarding dispositions but rather (certain sorts of) continuer-regarding dispositions. In other words, in spite of our deplorable tendencies to be selfish, it may be that *fundamentally* we are not self-interested at all but rather continuer-interested, where the relevant continuer relation can hold between oneself and another. That is one possibility. Another possibility, as we have just seen, is that what appears in the hypothetical examples to be continuer-interested behavior is really self-interested behavior, albeit at the experiential rather than at the theoretical level. I do not see how this latter possibility can be ruled out.

This result may seem to be a victory for traditionalists about what matters in survival. In a way it is. For on this latter possibility what matters primarily in survival is, after all, identity. But to whatever extent this result is a victory for traditionalists, it is a phyrric victory. For on the account under discussion the ultimate basis for our so-called egoistic survival values is an experiential illusion. The perceiver-self phenomenon involves our taking part of the content of our experience – what we have called the "observed" – and treating it as if it were the subject of our experience – the "observer." It isn't the subject of our experience.

So, does the realization that our egoistic survival values may be based on an illusion cause them to change? No. We may – almost surely will – continue to experience the perceiver-self phenomenon as an element of most of our experiences. But, now, almost as surely, we will not be able to respect the intuitions about our identity that this illusion encourages. And one of these intuitions, as we have seen, may well be that identity is primarily what matters in survival. Similar things could be said about the experiential belief that we are our bodies. This belief encourages the illusion that experiences in our phenomenal space somehow map naturally and straightforwardly onto their corresponding locations in physical space. They do not. And to the extent that the illusion that they do encourages our identification with our physical bodies, it too could easily warp our intuitions about what matters in survival and encourage the belief that identity is primarily what matters.

CONVERSING WITH THE DEAD

In classical times there was not really a problem of personal identity. Rather, there was a problem of death. The question of interest was not what secures our identities but whether bodily death is the end. Identity entered the discussion through the back door, in the service of answering this more pressing question. People feared death. However, many people also had intimations that bodily death is not the end. Even Plato, in *Phaedo,* remarks that in graveyards people sometimes see ghosts. So, from very early on, there are these two facts about the human condition: people fear death; and many people – probably, at any given time, most people – think that at least some people survive the demise of their gross physical bodies.

It is easy to understand how theorists, as well as ordinary people, might have assumed that if people survive their bodily deaths, there must be a vehicle for survival. However, even before the invention of the notion of an immaterial (unextended) soul, there was a ready vehicle available: fine matter. In classical times many Greeks apparently thought that the soul leaves the body when the person who dies expels his last breath, that it leaves his body in his breath, and perhaps even that it is that breath. It was Plato's genius (or perversity) to have suggested a *radical* alternative.

Although Plato never quite got the whole idea out, he suggested that the vehicle for survival was not any sort of physical object, not even breath, but, rather, an unextended thing. So far as we know, this suggestion was original to Plato (or Socrates). When others had talked of immaterial souls, they usually meant invisible, fine matter. Even Plato, in *Phaedo,* did not always distinguish sharply between something's being immaterial and its being invisible. But, then, sometimes he did seem to distinguish between these. How, then, if he did, did Plato ever arrive at the idea of an unextended soul? We do not know. He was concerned throughout *Phaedo* with the sources of generation and corruption. In his view, the corruption of a thing is brought about by its coming apart. He may have reasoned, as the good student of geometry that he was, that any extended thing, merely in virtue of its being extended, is potentially divisible and, hence, potentially corruptible. So, if people are incorruptible, they have to be unextended.

But why suppose that people are incorruptible and, hence, immortal? Plato may have thought he had evidence that people survive the demise of their gross physical bodies. But people would not have to be immortal to do that. In spite of Plato's arguments for immortality it is not clear why he thought that people are immortal. Nor is it clear why Aristotle, in spite of his more scientific turn of mind, followed Plato in making this assumption, at least for the rational part of the soul.

It is a little clearer why Plato thought it mattered whether people survive the demise of their gross physical bodies. Apparently he (or Socrates) thought that if people could get away from bodily distractions, it would help them get at the truth. And, Plato tells us that in one of Socrates' last thoughts, Socrates mused about the joys of conversing with the dead. Apparently, then, Plato (or Socrates) supposed that souls carried along with them their associated mental dispositions; and he thought that people were entitled to anticipate having the experiences of their postmortem selves.

A few centuries later, Lucretius wrote that the persistence of one's soul even together with one's mental dispositions would not entitle a person to anticipate having future experiences. In the context of his making the point that we have nothing to fear from bodily death, Lucretius argued that "if any feeling remains in mind or spirit after it has been torn from body, that is nothing to us, who are brought into being by the wedlock of body and spirit, conjoined and coalesced." He said that "even if the matter that composes us should be reassembled by time after our death and brought back into its present state," it still would "be no concern of ours once the chain of our identity had been snapped" (1951, Bk. 3). But why would it be of no concern?

Lucretius's answer, in effect, is that identity is a precondition of any such concern we might have for our continuers, and our identities terminate at our bodily deaths: "If the future holds travail and anguish in store, the self must be in existence, when that time comes, in order to experience it." "From this fate we are redeemed by death which denies existence to the self that might have suffered these tribulations." The moral of these reflections, Lucretius thought, is "that we have nothing to fear in death" since "one who no longer is cannot suffer, or differ in any way from one who has never been born, when once this mortal life has been usurped by death the immortal" (1951, Bk. 3). In sum, in Lucretius's view, regardless of what that is currently part of us persists and regardless of whether it is capable of having experiences and of performing actions, such as conversing with the dead, if it is not attended by our bodies, then it is not us, and if it is not us, then its experiences and actions are not something we can look forward to having and performing. Unfortunately, Lucretius did not argue for this view. He merely asserted it.

A question that in the West apparently did not arise in classical times is that of why the persistence either of one's soul, one's body, or *any* other underlying carrier is necessary for the persistence of one's mental dispositions (this question did arise, in a different context, in early Buddhist thought). We do not know how classical Western thinkers might have responded to this question. But there is an answer that might naturally suggest itself to anyone who thought about it. It is that the occurrent expressions of one's mental dispositions are individual mental episodes. These episodes come and go. It is a whole series of such transient episodes that collectively constitute what we normally regard as a person's occurrent mental life. Unless something were to underlie such a series it would be hard to explain both why it continued and, in case some such series did continue, why episodes included in it should be regarded as continuing the old series rather than as beginning new ones. In addition, it would be natural to assume that such a series could not sustain itself. So, it would have to be sustained by something else – something, ultimately, that could sustain itself. But what that could sustain one's occurrent mental states and their successors could also sustain itself? Before Plato's invention of the immaterial soul, all that was available to sustain occurrent mental states was matter. And that is what many people thought did sustain them: fine matter.

Plato, however, was convinced that the world of material objects is in constant flux. So, if the series of a person's occurrent mental states needs a sustainer because the various episodes of which it is composed come and go, shouldn't fine matter, for the same reason, also need a sustainer? After all, the various configurations into which matter gets assembled also come and go. The only things left to sustain the configurations of matter that might in turn sustain both series of peoples' occurrent mental states and the people themselves are immaterial souls. But if immaterial souls can sustain the material configurations that, in turn, are supposed to sustain a person's mental states, perhaps souls could sustain these mental states directly, without even working through matter. Plato may (or may not) have had some such thoughts. There is not a lot of textual evidence that he did but there is some. In any case, it would have been a natural thing for theorists to consider during the period from Plato to Locke.

Another possibility – at least in theory – is that the series of occurrent mental states continues without anything's sustaining it, that is, that it just continues. Contemplating that possibility, it seems, would lead one rather quickly to the question of what matters in survival. For if such a series were to continue, without anything else's playing the role of its sustainer, what would become of the person whose mental series it was in the first place? If the person does not continue, say, because he dies with the body, why should it matter to him in his concern to survive that his mental series continues? Apparently that's the question that Lucretius considered and answered that it should not matter. And if the person were to continue, even though the current constituents of her bodily and mental states did not continue, in what would her continuing consist? On this hypothesis, which has already discarded the notion of a sustainer of one's occurrent mental states, apparently a person's continuing would have to consist simply in the mental series itself continuing. By then, even if this hypothesis makes sense, why should the series' continuing matter? That is, why should earlier members of an occurrent bodily and/or mental series of episodic events, which do not themselves last, care whether they are followed by subsequent members of the series?

It does not really answer this question to reply, "So that they – the earlier members – can, say, converse with the dead." For on this hypothesis, while the conversation might continue, it is not clear that it would be the earlier members of the series who would continue it since they would no longer exist. And the person to whom these earlier members of the series belonged, if he continued at all, would continue the series only in a fictional sense – as the organizational category in terms of which we (i.e., bodily and/or mental episodes that are part of some current series) think about the series as a whole.

So far as we know, no one was to think such thoughts until at least the end of the seventeenth century; and no one was to hold them clearly in view until the end of the eighteenth. In the seventeenth century Spinoza and Locke may have thought them. Whether or not either of them did, Spinoza did not leave us with a theory of personal identity. And as we have seen, Locke was unclear on the point, although his theory of personal identity led other people, including Clarke, Collins, and Butler, to the brink of thinking such thoughts. It was not until the end of the eighteenth century, in the writings of Joseph Priestley, that a thinker finally crossed the threshold and the question of what matters in survival came clearly into view. Like Lucretius, Priestley was a scientific materialist. But, unlike Lucretius, Priestley believed that people survive their bodily deaths; at least he believed something close to that.

Priestley's written thoughts on what matters in survival emerged in the course of his considering an objection to his materialist views about survival of bodily death, an objection that he says was made to "the primitive Christians, as it may be at present" that "a proper resurrection is not only, in the highest degree, improbable, but even actually impossible since, after death, the body putrefies, and the parts that composed it are dispersed, and form other bodies, which have an equal claim to the same resurrection" (1778/1977, p. 165). So, Priestley imagined his critics asking where "can be the propriety of rewards and *punishments,* if the man that rises again be not identically the same with the man that acted and died?" (p. 165).

In reply, Priestly, first, made it clear, as if just for the record, that in his opinion "we shall be identically the same beings after the resurrection that we are at present." Then, "for the sake of those who may entertain a different opinion," he proposed to "speculate a little upon their hypothesis." His aim was to show that the hypothesis that we are not identical with any beings after the resurrection "is not inconsistent with a state of future rewards and punishments, and that it supplies motives sufficient for the regulation of our conduct here, with a view to it" (1778/1977, p. 165). In other words, Priestley's aim was to show that even if none of the people who will exist after our deaths are identical to any of us, it would not make

157

any difference since *identity is not what matters primarily in survival.* That this was Priestley's aim becomes especially clear when he continues:

> And metaphysical as the subject necessarily is, I do not despair of satisfying those who will give a due attention to it, that the propriety of rewards and punishments, with our hopes and fears derived from them, do not at all depend upon *such a kind of identity* as the objection that I have stated supposes. (p. 165; emphasis added)

So, Priestley, the materialist, asserted what Lucretius, the materialist, had denied. However, unlike Lucretius, Priestley argued for his view.

Priestley began his argument by distinguishing between "the identity of the man" and "the identity of the person." He, then, noted that it is only the identity of the person that is relevant to the present discussion. Next, he pointed out that even if people were to become convinced that over the course of a year there was a complete change, "though gradual and insensible," in the matter of which they were composed, it "would make no change whatever in our present conduct, or in our sense of obligation, respecting the duties of life, and the propriety of rewards and punishments; and consequently all hopes and fears, and expectations of every kind would operate exactly as before" (1778/1977, p. 166). The reason for this he said, is that "notwithstanding the complete change of the *man,* there would be no change of what I should call the *person*" (p. 166). Then, endorsing Locke, Priestley said that insofar as personal identity is requisite either for the propriety of rewards and punishments or for the concern that we take for our future selves, "the sameness and continuity of consciousness seems to be the only circumstance attended to by us." But as soon as he had gotten that out, Priestley went on to remark that, in his view, whether identity obtains is of no great consequence:

> Admitting, therefore, that the man consists wholly of matter, as much as the river does of water, or the forest of trees, and that this matter should be wholly changed in the interval between death and the resurrection; yet, if, after this state, we shall all *know one another again,* and *converse together as before,* we shall be, *to all intents and purposes,* the same persons. Our personal identity will be *sufficiently preserved,* and the expectation of it at present will have a proper influence on our conduct. (pp. 166–7; emphasis added)

This remarkable passage marks a theoretical breakthrough. So far as we know, no one previously, in the whole history of Western thought (Lucretius is the only serious competitor), had separated so clearly the question of whether we will be identical with someone who exists in the future from the question of whether it matters.

In considering whether it matters, Priestly separated three issues: first, the self-interested concerns that everyone has in their own futures; second, the concern that society as a whole has in the efficacy in motivating people to behave based on the prospect of future rewards and punishments; and, third, the concerns that Christian theologians, and Christians more generally, have in the propriety of divine rewards and punishments. Thus, toward the end of the eighteenth century Priestley introduced and embraced one of the key ideas – that identity is not primarily what matters in survival – that has been central to the revolution in personal identity theory in our own times. The worm had turned.

It was left to William Hazlitt, who was a student of Priestley's, to bring the question of what matters in survival to center stage. In his *Essay on the Principles of Human Action* (1805), Hazlitt asks how a theorist committed to the Lockean idea that one's identity extends as far as one's consciousness extends should respond "if that consciousness should be transferred to some other being?" How, Hazlitt asked, would such a person know that he had not been "imposed upon by a false claim of identity?" (1805/1969, pp. 135–6).

Hazlitt answered, on behalf of the Lockeans, that the idea of one's consciousness extending to someone else "is ridiculous": a person has "no other self than that which arises from this very consciousness." But, he countered, after our deaths,

> this self may be multiplied in as many different beings as the Deity may think proper to endue with the same consciousness; which if it can be so renewed at will in any one instance, may clearly be so in a hundred others. Am I to regard all these as equally myself? Am I equally interested in the fate of all? Or if I must fix upon some one of them in particular as my representative and other self, how am I to be determined in my choice? Here, then, I saw an end put to my speculations about absolute self-interest and personal identity. (1805/1969, p. 136)

Thus, Hazlitt saw that, hypothetically, one's consciousness might not continue in a single stream but instead might divide. And in asking *both* questions – "Am I to regard all of these as equally myself? Am I equally interested in the fate of all?" – he correctly separated the question of whether *identity* tracks continuity of consciousness from that of whether *self-concern* tracks it. Finally, in anticipation of what would not occur again to other philosophers until our own times, he concluded that because of the possibility of such a fission, neither identity nor self-concern necessarily tracks continuity of consciousness.

Hazlitt also used fission examples to call into question whether in cases in which there is no fission a person's present self-interest extends to his self in the future. First, he asked:

How then can this pretended unity of consciousness which is only reflected from the past, which makes me so little acquainted with the future that I cannot even tell for a moment how long it will be continued, whether it will be entirely interrupted by or renewed in me after death, and which might be multiplied in I don't know how many different beings and prolonged by complicated sufferings without my being any the wiser for it, how I say can a principle of this sort identify my present with my future interests, and make me as much a participator in what does not at all affect me as if it were actually impressed on my senses? (p. 138)

Hazlitt answered that it cannot:

It is plain, as this conscious being may be decompounded, entirely destroyed, renewed again, or multiplied in a great number of beings, and as, whichever of these takes place, it cannot produce the least alteration in my present being – that what I am does not depend on what I am to be, and that there is no communication between my future interests and the motives by which my present conduct must be governed. (pp. 138–9)

Finally, Hazlitt concluded:

I cannot, therefore, have a principle of active self-interest arising out of the immediate connection between my present and future self, for no such connection exists, or is possible . . . My personal interest in any thing must refer either to the interest excited by the actual impression of the object which cannot be felt before it exists, and can last no longer than while the impression lasts, or it may refer to the particular manner in which I am mechanically affected by the idea of my own impressions in the absence of the object. I can therefore have no proper personal interest in my future impressions . . . The only reason for my preferring my future interest to that of others, must arise from my anticipating it with greater warmth of present imagination. (pp. 139–40)

Hazlitt thus accomplished what, except for Priestley, others who had been sympathetic to Locke's views had resisted. He used fission examples, which previously others had employed only to criticize Locke, to motivate a view that went beyond Locke. Yet few noticed. Keats and Coleridge at least knew of Hazlitt's views, which were also mentioned in a few anonymous reviews, in one of them favorably (1806; 1835). But Hazlitt's views were never discussed in print by any philosopher that really mattered. Subsequently interest in the question of what matters in survival all but died (to be reborn in the late 1960s).

Throughout the nineteenth century spiritual substance accounts of the nature of self and of personal identity remained a respectable option. For instance, toward the end of the century, Sidgwick, in a passage that is reminiscent of Hazlitt and that may have influenced Parfit, briefly revived the question of whether identity matters in survival. Sidgwick wrote, "It must surely be admissible to ask the Egoist, 'Why should I sacrifice a present pleasure for a greater one in the future? Why should I concern myself about my own future feelings any more than about the feelings of other persons?'" (1907/1962, p. 418). He persisted:

> Grant that the Ego is merely a system of coherent phenomena, that the permanent identical "I" is not a fact but a fiction, as Hume and his followers maintain; why, then, should one part of the series of feelings into which the Ego is resolved be concerned with another part of the same series, any more than with any other series? (p. 418)

But without the prod of fission examples Sidgwick managed to set this question aside.

From the beginning of the twentieth century until the 1960s, most personal identity theorists assumed that some sort of relational view of personal identity must be correct. The main question that interested them was that of whether physical or psychological relations were essential to a person's persistence, and then, depending on how they answered, which physical or psychological relations were essential. It was not until the early 1970s, primarily in the work of Shoemaker (1970) and Parfit (1971), that the question of what matters in survival made a dramatic comeback. Now that this question is back, what will become of it? What should become of it?

Today, in the view of many thinkers, our bodies, or at least the physical mechanisms (or appropriately related physical descendants of these mechanisms) that underlie our consciousness, must persist continuously for us to persist. These mechanisms are the vehicle for the preservation of one's identity, which in turn is widely regarded as a precondition of a person's obtaining what matters in survival. Even those who take the view that identity is not what matters primarily in survival usually insist only that one's physical persistence can be thinner than traditionalists are willing to allow and yet still ensure that what matters in survival is obtained. For instance, in the case of teletransportation, where during the transmission all that is preserved of a person is physically encoded information sufficient to enable a qualitatively similar replica to be reassembled later, traditionalists and radicals differ over whether the person who initiates the process obtains what matters in survival. Yet members of both groups of theorists tend to assume that, at every moment, there must be some physical continuer or other of the original person that underlies and sustains some privileged part of her mentality in order for her to obtain what matters in survival. Thus, in effect, physical continuers have replaced immaterial souls as the vehicles, if not of our survival, then at least of what matters in our survival. In other words, in the opinion of almost all theorists, our values, if not our identities, must be anchored somewhere: It is not enough just for the conversation to go on. What is not so clear, however, is why it is not enough.

References

Anonymous. 1806. Review of William Hazlitt's *An Essay on the Principles of Human Action*. *British Critic* 38:536–48.

——— 1835. Hazlitt's First Essay. *Monthly Repository* 9:480–5

Ayers, Michael.1991. *Locke,* 2 vols. New York: Routledge.

Baillie, James. 1993. *Problems in Personal Identity*. New York: Paragon.

Barresi, John. 1994. Morton Prince and B.C.A.: A Historical Footnote on the Confrontation Between Dissociation Theory and Freudian Psychology in a Case of Multiple Personality. In *Psychological Concepts and Dissociation Disorders,* ed. R. Klein and B. Doane, pp. 85–129. Hillsdale, N.J.: Erlbaum.

Beahrs, John.1982. *Unity and Multiplicity*. New York: Brunner-Mazel.

Beck, Charlotte Joko. 1993. *Nothing Special*. San Francisco: Harper.

Behan, David P. 1979. Locke on Persons and Personal Identity. *Canadian Journal of Philosophy* 9:53–75.

Berger, Peter. 1963. *An Invitation to Sociology*. New York: Doubleday.

Borges, Jorge Luis. 1962. Borges and I. Trans. James E. Irby, from *Labyrinths: Selected Stories and other Writings,* ed. Donald A. Yates and James E. Irby. New York: New Directions.

Braude, Stephen. 1990. Selected Poems of Patience Worth. In *New Directions in Prose and Poetry 40,* ed. J. Laughlin, pp. 161–2. New York: New Directions.

Butler, Joseph. 1736. *The Analogy of Religion, Natural and Revealed*. Reprinted 1852. London: Henry G. Bohn.

Clark, Thomas W. 1996. Death, Nothingness, and Subjectivity. In *The Experience of Philosophy,* ed. D. Kolak and R. Martin, 3rd ed., pp. 481–90. Belmont, Calif.: Wadsworth.

Clarke, Samuel. 1738. *The Works of Samuel Clarke,* 4 vols. Reprinted 1928. New York: Garland.

Donagan, Alan.1990. Real Persons. *Logos* 11:1–16.

Eisenberg, Nancy. 1982. *The Development of Prosocial Behavior*. New York: Academic.

Engler, Jack. 1986. Therapeutic Aims in Psychotherapy and Meditation. In *Transformations of Consciousness,* ed. K. Wilber, J. Engler, and D. P. Brown, pp. 17–52. Boston: Shambhala.

Frankfurt, Harry G. 1971. Freedom of the Will and the Concept of a Person. *Journal of Philosophy* 68:5–20.

Hanley, Richard. 1993. On Valuing Radical Transformation. *Pacific Philosophical Quarterly* 74:209–20.

Hazlitt, William. 1805. *Essay on the Principles of Human Action and some Remarks on the Systems of Hartley and Helvetius*. Reprinted 1969, with an introduction by John R. Nabholtz. Gainesville, Fla.: Scholars' Facsimiles & Reprints.

Hilgard, Ernest. 1977. *Divided Consciousness*. New York: Wiley. Expanded edition, 1986. Reprinted 1991, in part, in *Self and Identity*, ed. D. Kolak and R. Martin, eds., pp. 89–114. New York: Macmillan.

James, William.1890. *The Principles of Psychology*, 2 vols. New York: Holt. Reprinted 1950. New York: Dover.

  1902. *The Varieties of Religious Experience*. New York: Longman's, Green.

Jencks, Christopher. 1990. Varieties of Altruism. In *Beyond Self-Interest,* ed. Jane J. Mansbridge, pp. 54–67. Chicago: University of Chicago Press.

Jung, Carl. 1961. *Memories, Dreams, Reflections*. Recorded and ed. Aniela Jaffe, trans. R. Winston and C. Winston. New York: Pantheon.

Kolak, Daniel, and Raymond Martin. 1987. Personal Identity and Causality: Becoming Unglued. *American Philosophical Quarterly* 24:339–47.

Krishnamurti, Jiddu. 1969. *Freedom from the Known,* ed. Mary Lutyens. New York: Harper & Row.

  1997. *Reflections on the Self,* ed. Raymond Martin. Chicago: Open Court.

Law, Edmund. 1823. A Defense of Mr. Locke's Opinion Concerning Personal Identity. In John Locke (1823/1963), III.177–201.

Lewis, David. 1976. Survival and Identity. In *The Identities of Persons,* ed. Amelie Rorty, pp.17–40. Berkeley: University of California Press.

  1983. Postscript to "Survival and Identity." In *Philosophical Papers*, vol. 1. New York: Oxford University Press.

Locke, John. 1694. *An Essay Concerning Human Understanding,* ed., Peter H. Nidditch. Oxford: Clarendon Press, 1975.

  1823. *The Works of John Locke,* 10 vols. London: Thomas Tegg. Reprinted 1963. Hildesheim, Germany: Scientia Verlag Aalan.

Lucretius. 1951. *De Rerum Natura,* trans. R. E. Latham. Harmondsworth: Penguin.

Mansbridge, Jane J. 1990. The Rise and Fall of Self-Interest in the Explanation of Political Life. In *Beyond Self-Interest* ed. Jane J. Mansbridge, pp. 3–22. Chicago: University of Chicago Press.

Martin, C. B., and Max Deutscher. 1966. Remembering. *Philosophical Review* 75:161–97.

Martin, Raymond. 1987. Memory, Connecting, and What Matters in Survival. *Australasian Journal of Philosophy* 65:82–97. Reprinted 1993. In *Personal Identity,* ed. Harold W. Noonan, pp. 337–52. Hampshire: Dartmouth.

  1988. Identity's Crisis. *Philosophical Studies* 53:207–21.

1991. Identity, Transformation, and What Matters in Survival. In *Self and Identity*, ed. D. Kolak and R. Martin, pp. 289–301. New York: Macmillan.

1992. Self-Interest and Survival. *American Philosophical Quarterly* 29:165–84.

1993a. *Having* the Experience: The Next Best Thing to Being There. *Philosophical Studies* 70:63–79.

1993b. Real Values. *Metaphilosophy* 24:400–6.

1995. Fission Rejuvenation. *Philosophical Studies* 72:17–40.

Martin, Raymond, and John Barresi. 1995. Hazlitt on the Future of the Self. *Journal of the History of Ideas* 56:463–81.

Martin, Raymond, John Barresi, and Alessandro Giovannelli. Forthcoming. Fission Examples in the Eighteenth and Early Nineteenth Century Personal Identity Debate. *History of Philosophy Quarterly*.

Morrison, Tony. 1973. *Sula*. New York: Knopf. Reprinted 1982. New York: Signet.

Nagel, Thomas. 1986. *The View from Nowhere*. New York: Oxford University Press.

Nozick, Robert. 1981. *Philosophical Explanations*. Cambridge, Mass.: Harvard University Press.

Nyanamoli, B., Ed. and trans. 1976. *Visuddhimagga: The Path of Purification by Buddhaghosha*, 2 vols. Boulder: Shambhala.

Parfit, Derek. 1971. Personal Identity. *Philosophical Review*, 80: 3–27.

1984. *Reasons and Persons*. Oxford: Clarendon Press.

Perry, John. 1972. Can the Self Divide? *Journal of Philosophy* 69: 463–88.

1976. The Importance of Being Identical. In *The Identities of Persons*, ed. Amelie Rorty, pp. 67–90. Berkeley: University of California Press.

1978. *A Dialogue Concerning Personal Identity and Immortality*. Indianapolis, Ind.: Hackett.

Persson, Ingmar. 1996. The Involvement of Our Identity in Experimental Memory. In Persson, *Neither Persons nor Human Beings*, pp. 16–34. Lund, Sweden: Lund Philosophy Reports.

Priestley, Joseph. 1777. *Disquisitions Relating to Matter and Spirit and the Doctrine of Philosophical Necessity Illustrated*. Reprinted 1976. New York: Garland.

Priestley, Joseph, and Richard Price. 1778. *A Free Discussion of the Doctrines of Materialism, and Philosophical Necessity, In a Correspondence Between Dr. Price and Dr. Priestley*. Reprinted 1977. Millwood, N.Y.: Kraus.

Reid, Thomas. 1785. *Essay on the Intellectual Powers of Man*. In *The Works of Thomas Reid*, ed. William Hamilton, 6th ed. Edinburgh: MacIachlan and Stewart, 1863.

Rescher, Nicholas. 1992–4. *A System of Pragmatic Idealism*, 3 vols. Princeton, N.J.: Princeton University Press.

Rousseau, Jean-Jacques. 1969. *Les confessions*. In *Oeuvres complètes*, vol. 1, ed. B. Gagnebin and Marcel Raymond. Paris: Gallimard.

Rovane, Carol. 1990. Branching Self-Consciousness. *Philosophical Review,* 99:355–95.

Sacks, Oliver. 1985. *The Man Who Mistook His Wife for a Hat.* New York: Harper & Row.

1995. *An Anthropologist on Mars.* New York: Knopf.

Sartre, Jean-Paul. 1966. *Being and Nothingness,* trans. Hazel E. Barnes. New York: Washington Square Press.

Shoemaker, Sydney. 1970. Persons and Their Pasts. *American Philosophical Quarterly* 7:269–85.

1984. Personal Identity: A Materialist Account. In *Personal Identity,* ed. Sydney Shoemaker and Richard Swinburne, pp. 69–152. Oxford: Basil Blackwell.

Sidgwick, Henry. 1907. *The Methods of Ethics* (1874), 7th ed. Reprinted 1962. Chicago: University of Chicago Press.

Sosa, Ernest. 1990. Surviving Matters. *Nous* 24:305–30.

Taylor, Richard. 1963. *Metaphysics,* 2nd ed. Englewood Cliffs, N.J.: Prentice-Hall.

Tucker, Abraham. 1763. *Man in Quest of Himself.* Reprinted 1984. In *Metaphysical Tracts by English Philosophers of the Eighteenth Century,* ed. S. Parr. Hildesheim, Germany: Georg Olms.

1768–77. *The Light of Nature Pursued,* 7 vols., 1805 ed. Reprinted 1977. New York: Garland.

Unger, Peter. 1991. *Identity, Consciousness, and Value.* New York: Oxford University Press.

Vajiranana, P. 1975. *Buddhist Meditation in Theory and Practice.* Lumpur: Buddhist Missionary Society.

Voltaire. 1734. *Traite de metaphysique.* Reprinted 1937. Ed., H. T. Patterson. Manchester: Manchester University Press.

White, Stephen. 1989. Metapsychological Relativism and the Self. *Journal of Philosophy* 86:298–323.

Wiggins, David. 1967. *Identity and Spatio-Temporal Continuity.* Oxford: Basil Blackwell.

Wilkes, Kathleen. 1988. *Real People.* Oxford: Clarendon Press.

Williams, Bernard. 1970. The Self and the Future. *Philosophical Review* 79:161–80.

Index

169